Heart and Soul

Heart and Soul

An Inspiring Collection of Light Verse
on Life, Love, Faith, and the Military

Jack London Riehl

iUniverse, Inc.
New York   Bloomington

Heart and Soul
An Inspiring Collection of Light Verse on Life, Love, Faith, and the Military

Copyright © 2010 by Jack London Riehl

All rights reserved. No part of this book may be used or reproduced by any means, graphic, electronic, or mechanical, including photocopying, recording, taping or by any information storage retrieval system without the written permission of the publisher except in the case of brief quotations embodied in critical articles and reviews.

The views expressed in this work are solely those of the author and do not necessarily reflect the views of the publisher, and the publisher hereby disclaims any responsibility for them.

iUniverse books may be ordered through booksellers or by contacting:

iUniverse
1663 Liberty Drive
Bloomington, IN 47403
www.iuniverse.com
1-800-Authors (1-800-288-4677)

Because of the dynamic nature of the Internet, any Web addresses or links contained in this book may have changed since publication and may no longer be valid.

ISBN: 978-1-4502-3182-4 (sc)
ISBN: 978-1-4502-3183-1 (ebk)

Printed in the United States of America

iUniverse rev. date: 8/27/2010

About the Cover

Evergreen Lake is a beautiful, private lake that, for many years, was owned and developed by the author. He wrote many poems there. It has two and a half miles of shoreline and seventeen acres of crystal clear water. Because it is on the Mississippi flyway, a variety of ducks and geese visit it in waterfowl season. Its name was also chosen as a companion name to the Riehl family home place, Evergreen Heights in Godfrey, Illinois.

Another view, at sunset, of the forty-four-foot-deep Evergreen Lake pictured on the cover.

To the glory of God

and

dedicated

to my dear wife, Carol

Magic Pen

I've always had a problem, friends,
In case you haven't heard,
A most unusual problem, this—
Concerning written word.
Sometimes it is a blessing, and
Sometimes it is a curse;
You see, I have this magic pen,
That always writes in verse!

Ambition

A scepter for the king of state,
An eagle plume for poet great—
But not for dreamers such as I,
Just an ordinary guy;
Yet ruler of a realm I'd be,
The realm of *doubtful* poetry.
A feather, too, for this poor king—
Plucked from the lowly chicken's wing!

Contents

About the Cover v

    Magic Pen ix
    Ambition. x

Thanks to xv

Foreword xvii

Preface xxiii

    Dreaming xxiv
    The End of Day xxiv

I. Family 1

    To Mom 3
    Mother 6
    Mom's Message 7
    Love Note 8
    Mom Again 9
    Dad 10

II. Friends 13

    Friend 14
    Hugs 15
    Milton 16
    Poor Joe 19

III. How Time Flies! 21

    Calendar Poems 22
    Gardens 26
    Siege of the Seasons 30
    Caw 33
    Warm Colors 36

    Christmas Is a Magic Time 37
    Choir Rehearsal. 39
    Christmas Anthems. 40
    Christmas Thanks 42
    After Christmas. 42

IV. The Sharing. 43

    The Sharing. 44
    Love-Talk 46
    Goddess 47
    Cheer Up 48
    The Cure. 49

V. Jack's War 51

    Travelogue (St. Louis to Sacramento) 52
    My Chapel 54
    The Dit-Dah Blues 56
    The G. B. (Goldbrick) 57
    A Soldier's Dilemma 58
    Precipitation 59
    The Rumor Monger 60
    No Paper Doll 61
    I'm Dreaming 62
    Pfc. 64
    Corporal 66
    Sergeants. 67
    Louies 69
    Rank. 70
    Where Go My Clothes?. 71
    Poison. 72
    On GI Biscuits (or "Ingenuity") 73
    On Bully-Beef. 73
    "The Chow in This Unit Is Terrible!" (A Story) 74
    Signs. 75
    Government Issue (GI) 76
    Beachhead. 77
    Air Raid 79

    Sniper 81
    Aussies. 83
    Reminiscing 85
    The Saga of 'Nam 88

VI. The Lighter Side 91

    Wolf 92
    Pianos 93
    Chiropractor 94
    Pigs 96
    Cheetah. 98
    Mother-in-Law 99
    Mashed Taters and Squirrel Gravy 102

VII. Finding Love Again 105

    Autumn Love 106
    Miracle! 108
    The Gift 109
    Tears 110
    You 112
    Yours 113
    Proposal 114
    Rainbow's End 115
    Carol 116
    My World Is Where You Are 118
    Home 119
    Tina-Dog 121

VIII. School Days 125

    The Librarian 126
    Subbing. 127
    Swan Song 129

IX. Fields and Streams 131

    Fish-Bit 132
    Trout Fisherman 133

    The Hunter's Reward............................137
    Dove Hunter..................................137

X. Armchair Philosopher................................139

    Eagles..140
    Gossip..141
    Four-Letter Words.............................142
    Pronouns.....................................143
    The Surgeon's Prayer..........................144
    Fashion......................................145
    Book of Life..................................146
    Key to Happiness.............................148

XI. Heart and Soul.....................................151

    My God......................................152
    Have Faith....................................153
    Pioneers......................................154
    Foundations..................................154
    Above All....................................155
    God Bless You................................156
    Microscopic...................................157
    He's There!...................................158
    Rainbow Song.................................159
    Look Up!.....................................160
    Tomorrow (A New Beginning) 162
    Long Hunter..................................163
    Hymn of Creation.............................165

XII. Over the Hill.....................................167

    Old-Timer....................................168
    Has-Been 169
    Think Young.................................171

About the Author......................................172

Thanks to

Renee Chavez, for her hard work, sensitivity, and expertise,

and to

John Mitchell Wilson,
for his generous time and technical support.

Foreword

In the 1890s, Walter A. Riehl (pronounced Reel) was a local, amateur heavyweight boxer in Alton, Illinois. He was chosen to fight an exhibition fight with the world heavyweight champion, Bob Fitzsimmons, whose tour of America took him to that small Illinois town. This exhibition bout heightened Walter's interest in boxing.

Records show that on October 28, 1899, the British-born Fitzsimmons was booked to fight in Tattershall, Illinois (near Chicago). It is believed that Jack Riehl's father, Walter, made the long trip to the windy city area for this fight.

Walter was born unable to hear a birdsong or a clap of thunder or the bell in the boxing ring that always starts off every round. Walter arrived late only to find a rugged, muscular-looking man sitting in his seat. He could not hear or understand the other man's words, but could see him jabbing his thumb at the seat number on his own ticket stub. It was the same number as Walter's ticket number.

The fight was sold out; obviously there were two tickets with the same seat number, one a counterfeit made by an unscrupulous ticket scalper. Walter had traveled a long way, and the cost of the ticket had set him back quite a bit financially. He did not know or care who the man was, but, being a heavyweight fighter, he confidently took off his coat and prepared to punch the stranger in the nose. Before the two men actually came to blows, boxing fans seated nearby seemed to realize Walter was deaf and wrote him a note. Only then did Walter realize he was preparing to punch in the nose the famous novelist Jack London.

During the fight, the two men shared the no-longer-disputed seat on the bench. After the fight, Walter Riehl and Jack London went out to a nearby steakhouse to enjoy a steak dinner together and afterward corresponded.

Walter and Caroline Riehl's first baby was a girl they named (Betty) Jane. When a second child, a son, came along on May 19, 1922 in Godfrey, Illinois, Walter and Caroline fortuitously named him Jack London Riehl, after Walter's famous writer-friend.

Walter completed his schooling only through the fourth grade because of his hearing disability. (In those days, there were no special education programs.) However, he was a voracious reader and had a library of hundreds and hundreds of books. Jack inherited his father's love of books and of good literature.

Like *Jack London*, the well-known author and adventurer, his namesake, *Jack London Riehl*, has also been a writer and adventurer. He was accidentally and almost fatally shot at age thirteen by careless older boys who were playing with a .22 rifle.

Jack began writing in his high-school years, the first of a lifetime of poetry. He wrote his first two poems at age eighteen with his rhyming "magic pen." He has been much in demand for writing humorous roasts for friends and relatives, special occasions, celebrations, and formal dedications. He has written song lyrics, one of which was set to music by recording artist Tim Hayden and sung by country music singer Jim Ed Brown.

A love of working the land is also a Riehl family trait. Grandfather Riehl was a nationally renowned horticulturalist; Jack's daughter, Carol Ann Riehl, hybridizes daylilies and has registered many of them, one of which she named *Jack London Riehl*. Jack's mother, Caroline, owned a florist shop in St. Louis and was president of the St. Louis Retail Florist Association for many years. Born into this family of horticulturalists, Jack has been a naturalist and conservationist all of his life (and weaves these deep convictions into his poetry). He is the last of a line of three generations of nurserymen.

Never in the ring before, the author literally fought his way into Army combat duty by fighting a professional boxer to prove he was not handicapped by a minor impairment on his left hand. He served in World War II with the 7th Cavalry Regiment, 1st Division, guarding

General Douglas MacArthur's headquarters and family in the U. S. Embassy in Tokyo, Japan. After graduating from OCS (officer candidate school), he was second lieutenant/investigating officer of court-martial cases for all allied troops in Brisbane, Australia. He was called back into the Korean War (Army Enlisted Reserves) to train other officers in Indiantown Gap, Pennsylvania.

Loving horses but never having owned one, he rented a horse from a riding stable while he was assigned to take an enlisted reserve training program in Colorado. He taught himself to ride and rode in the mountains when off duty, later purchasing four riding horses for his Illinois farm and lake property. He developed the lake property into a commercial fishing venture (now closed), and for many years he made his own fishing lures and bow and arrows for hunting.

Jack comes from a spiritually-oriented family in which, traditionally, there have been teachers and missionaries. At one time, he considered going into the ministry, and later on, became a lay speaker in the United Methodist Church. But he chose teaching as his profession and taught high-school English for thirty-three years in St. Louis, Missouri (Normandy District). After retiring, he was a substitute teacher for another five years.

Though called "Coach Riehl," he was actually the *playing captain* of the Middle Tennessee Intermediate Tennis League of Donelson, Tennessee. It has been said that, for ten years, his tennis team won more trophies than any other team in the history of the local YMCA. The author also won a dozen or more individual trophies and plaques. He won numerous Senior Olympics medals and ribbons. He played tennis and worked a half-acre church garden ministry until he was almost eighty-two years old.

Over the years, Jack developed a poetic style reminiscent of James Whitcomb Riley and Edgar A. Guest; at other times his poetry brings to mind Ogden Nash. He excels at light verse and strong expressions of faith typical of what Tom Brokaw called *the greatest generation's* love of God and country. His poetry appeals to the young and the old, men and women. He proves, as did poet Carl Sandburg in "Chicago" and today's more modern poets, that poetry is for men too, not just for women and lovers.

He has begun work on a new novel titled *Jack's War*, an autobiography paralleling the military chapter from "Jack's War" in *Heart and Soul*.

Heart and Soul is a book of light verse about life, love, faith, and the military into which Jack has poured out *his* heart and soul.

Carol M. (Lefmann) Riehl, author's wife

Note: Confusing as it is, Jack's mother was named Caroline; his daughter is Carol; and his wife is Carol.

American novelist and adventurer, Jack London, depicted on U.S. Postage Stamp issued in 1986, from a sketch by California artist Richard C. Sparks. Novelist London is well known for serialized novels The Call of the Wild *(1903) and* White Fang *(1906).*
© 1986 USPS. All rights reserved.

Preface

During my senior year at Roosevelt High School in St. Louis, Missouri, I was a member of Bwana, the yearbook staff. The teacher who sponsored these classes informed the students early in the year that they were required to contribute an article before the publication's deadline.

Typical high-school teenager that I was, I procrastinated until the night before the deadline. That night, in front of the fireplace, I painstakingly composed two short poems entitled "Dreaming" and "The End of Day." When the yearbook came out, I was amazed to find both of these poems in it; these were the first two poems I had ever written.

-JLR

Dreaming

I love to lie before the hearth
But soon my drowsy eyelids close,
And the cheery flames die fast.
When suddenly I awaken,
My dreams are tossed away,
For there before my tired eyes
Are ashes—cold and gray!

The End of Day

The sun has set and in the west,
The ruddy glow fades fast;
The birds and bees have gone to rest,
And lights dim shadows cast.
The flowers bow their weary heads,
The flush of day is past;
The shades of twilight deepen,
And night has come at last.

1939

I. Family

Mother Caroline and Jack (approximately three years old).

To Mom

I remember so well and yet I know
That it was very long ago;
With the love-light in her eyes—
Her soft voice humming lullabies;
I see her there beside my bed;
I feel her hand upon my head,
Like an angel kneeling there,
Listening to my evening prayer;
And we were as close, as close could be—
My mother and *me*!

My heart is full of a thousand thoughts
That mere words can't begin to say,
But I want you to know that I love you,
And that I remember it's Mother's Day!

    Your son

13 May, 1945 – Milne Bay, New Guinea

Young Jack sailing his homemade boat in his mother's lily pool on their farm, called Flower Field Farm, in Godfrey, Illinois, where the family grew peonies commercially.

Mother Caroline and father Walter.

Jack on fence at Flower Field Farm.

Mother

Most precious word, blessed from above,
So soothing and so full of love . . .
Mother—Mother.
You brought us to the light of day
And guided us along life's way—
Always there to dry our tears
And comfort us through all our fears . . .
Mother—Mother.

Fed us, bathed us, helped us dress—
You held us close against your breast;
Helped us say our prayers at night—
Taught us to tell wrong from right.
Mother—Mother.

Cleaned up every mess we made,
Forgave us always when we strayed.
Together we survived the teens,
The high-school and the college scenes.
Mother—Mother.

How great your love these long years through—
How great our love returned to you;
Knowing always that you cared,
Treasuring the joys we shared.
Mother—Mother.

Problems, trials you saw us through,
As teacher, nurse, and counselor too.
You sacrificed in every way and
Loved us like no other.
No other word is half so sweet
Or half so dear as *mother*!
Mother—Mother—Mother.

Set to music by recording artist Tim Hayden, Ned's Place Recording Studio, Nashville, Tennessee.

Mom's Message

Why sit you there with thoughts so far apart,
With sad face and even sadder heart?
Have you so little faith to think our love is through?
I did not say, "Good-bye," but just "Adieu."
So smile—shed not a single tear;
Instead, rejoice to know I'm happy here!
Reunited with dear friends, departed long ago—
To you I said, "Adieu," to them, "Hello."

We've so much to say, these friends and I,
And they'll lead me through the gardens, bye and bye.
If you, these birds could hear—these flowers see,
I truly believe you would all envy me.
This place, these friends, my fondest dreams fulfill;
Remember too—I am your friend and mother still!

I dearly loved the notes and cards you all did send
And hate to think our conversations now might end,
So anytime we've precious thoughts to share,
Let's simply carry on our little talks—in prayer.
I promise you I'll always keep in touch—
You see, things really haven't changed so much.

That's all for now . . . not that I've run out of words,
But it's time to take that garden walk and feed my birds.
So grieve not, but go live, love, work, and play;
Doubt not our hands, as well as hearts, shall touch again one day.
Until that time, know that my soul is free!
Go now, and share with others all the love you gave to me!

Love Note

Dear friends and family,
    Grieve not for me.
Here, in this world beyond,
    A universal bond
Still links me to you there . . .
    A bond called prayer.

Perhaps you're thinking now
    Just when or how
You could have said or shown,
    Or if I could have known,
The love I had from you.
    Indeed . . . I knew!

This message now I send . . .
    Death does not end
The things we hold most dear
    But just those things we fear;
No hate, pain, worry now,
    But *love* lives on.

Mom Again

For Bernice, my new mother-in-law.

My mother passed long years ago
To gardens up above;
She left behind for all she knew
A legacy of love.
A few small bonds, a modest house—
(Some folks would look askance).
The wealth of love she left I deem
A rich inheritance.

And I remember other things:
Her flowers and her birds;
The cookies baked at Christmastime,
Her softly spoken words.
So many precious things I've missed
Since Mom went on her way,
And they're recalled so vividly
Each year at Mother's Day.

But now, you see, I'm married to
A lady I adore—
Her mother is a darling too . . .
I have a *Mom* once more!

Dad

(From son)

I remember . . .
    How you bounced me on your knee,
Telling stories there to me;
    Taught me how to bat and bunt—
How to drive and fish and hunt;
    Cheered me up when I was sad
And scolded me when I was bad;
    Briefed me on the facts of life—
Counseled me through teenage strife;
    Stood there beside me, filled with pride,
Beaming, as I took a bride.

(From daughter)

I remember . . .
    When I was small you called me mouse—
Made me a princess in your house;
    Brought me ribbons for my hair—
Called me your fairest of the fair;
    Teased me with a playful joke—
Fixed my dolly when she broke.
    The proudest man I've ever seen . . .
Your princess was homecoming queen!
    Though grown and married now, you see,
Your princess, I will always be.

(From both)

We remember . . .
    Through thick and thin we always knew
We had support and love from you.
    We, in return, our love avow . . .
Our love was then—our love is now!

The truest friend we've ever had . . .
Father . . . Papa . . . Daddy . . . Dad!

Written April 7, 1989
Set to music by recording artist Tim Hayden, February, 2010.

II. Friends

Friend

What is a friend? Why, that's one who
Can cheer you up when you are blue—
By simply being near awhile,
Converts your frown into a smile;
Who understands, forgives mistakes,
And always gives more than he takes;
And when dark clouds ofttimes appear,
Is there with sympathetic ear.
Oh, lucky you, to have a friend
On whom you always can depend;
A friend like that, for whom to care—
A friend like that, with whom to share!
A gift most precious, all your own,
Who loves you for yourself alone.
God's dearest gift, a gift of love,
Sent down directly from above.
Accept this gift, abuse it never—
Protect and cherish it forever!

1992

Hugs

Hugs are really something!
Hugs are really sweet!
Hugs are so relaxing!
Hugs just can't be beat!

Hugs are very special,
And not just for your date—
Hug your family and your friends—
Hugs are really great!
Some hug so very gently,
And others like to squeeze
Until you're white and breathless,
And you buckle at the knees.

Though techniques of huggers vary,
One thing is always true—
Hugging, in 'most any form,
Brings pleasure, through and through!
A hug is, oh, so wonderful!
But you already knew it;
The time for action has arrived—
No more talking . . . *Do it*!

Milton

To Milton Sanford

I never heard him say an unkind word
    Or voice an unclean thought;
Such things as these are tributes to
    The way that he was taught.
Farm-born in those depression years,
    He grew up used to toil.
He liked to saw and split stove wood
    And loved to work God's soil.
It was plain he loved God's works around him,
    Not shown, perhaps, in words,
But clearly shown, instead, in actions—
    Caring daily for God's birds.
So many kindly things he did,
    And did 'most every day;
What's more, these things he seemed to do
    In such an unassuming way.
If you were in his presence
    Just for a little while,
Some simple thing he'd say or do
    Would surely bring a smile.
He lived according to those laws
    Passed down from up above—
So freely offering help to friends.
    So generous with love!
Husband, father, grandpa, neighbor, friend—
    We miss him so today,
But do not dwell in grief too long.
    This would not be his way!
For love goes on, for him and us,
    One thing I surely know—
He's smiling now and we should too,
    For he would have it so!

You see, he is not really gone, for
    Love is as eternal as God, himself.

April 5, 1992

The author and friend Milton Sanford worked a half-acre garden, with all proceeds from their ministry used to help people in the church and community who were unable to pay their medical bills. Milton died a year later and author worked the garden alone for another fifteen or twenty years. Photograph by Marta Aldrich, United Methodist Reporter, *August 30, 1991.*

Poor Joe

To my good friend, Joe L.

Now those of us who know you best
    All know that you're a louse;
Not one of us suspected, though,
    Pal Joey was a souse!
I'm sure that others in our group
    Occasionally imbibe,
But you've invited, by this stunt,
    Pure, unrelenting jibe!
Forget the golf and tennis now
    And try to learn to knit . . .
Whoops! Guess that knitting's out
    Since you can't even sit!
Perhaps you think this overkill,
    My raising all this fuss.
You must admit this stunt you pulled
    Is quite ridiculous!
My backhand, I admit is weak,
    But listen, you old fool . . .
I never once, in all my life,
    Fell off a barroom stool!
I know I've laid it on quite thick
    And hope you'll not be bitter;
Next time don't hesitate to call
    On me—your *designated sitter*!

February 25, 1995

III. How Time Flies!

Calendar Poems

January

The time has come to face once more
    That ancient institution,
Which once a year so many make . . .
    The New Year's resolution.
I often have some problems here—
    To make them's not so rough;
I write a long list every year . . .
    It's *keeping* them that's tough!

February

Now leap year plays some strange tricks on
    Those born on twenty-nine;
You *miss* these birthdays as a kid,
    But when you're grown, it's fine.
The *ladies* born upon this day
    Are happy, for you see,
All of them are just *one-fourth*
    As old as they should be!

March

Look up! The days are warming fast,
    And spring is on its way;
Perhaps we'll see a bit of green
    Before St. Patrick's Day.
Amazing . . . how on this one day,
    A day of fun and cheer,
Out from behind each tree and rock,
    Those Irish will appear!

April

I love the clean, fresh odor of
    Those showers in the spring,
And each small touch of beauty that
    The first wild flowers bring.
I love the thoughts of Easter Day . . .
    That Christ had died and thus,
Because he rose on Easter morn,
    His promise is for us!

May

Two very, very special days,
    We celebrate in May;
On one, we honor dear old Mom—
    We call it Mother's Day.
Memorial Day's the other one,
    To most, a day of play,
But actually, in memory
    Of loved ones passed away.

June

Once more that old familiar shout:
    School's out! School's out!
For teachers, the end of joy and grief—
    From them, just sighs of pure relief!
And also heard both far and wide,
    Those famous words, "Here comes the bride!"
He stands already in the room.
    Why don't they sing, "There stands the groom!"?

July

Now here's a month that truly starts
    Off with a bang, I'd say.
Americans all know *the fourth*
    As Independence Day.
The kids look forward to this day,
    For fireworks delight 'em;
Loud—exciting—lovely, but . . .
    Be careful when you light 'em!

August

Most folks I know spend August
    Just trying to stay cool
And envying their neighbors
    Who have a swimming pool.
They say that these are *dog days*,
    But I don't hear no barkin'
And I've observed that young folks
    Sure do a lot of sparkin'.
Back seats of cars get lots of use
    Around here every night,
Especially when the air is clear,
    And the moon is shining bright.

September

September is a month of change—
    From hot and dry, to cool,
As frantic mothers everywhere
    Prepare their kids for school.
The birds head south to winter homes,
    Inspiring fools like me,
To take up pen and to inscribe
    This simple poetry.

October

God takes his brush and palette up—
    Rich reds and golds unfurled;
Once more he shows his artistry—
    His canvas . . . all the world!
But to the kids, October is
    A black and orange scene;
It's goblin time and trick or treat . . .
    October's Halloween!

November

November is the gourmet month;
    Thanksgiving Day is near,
With turkey, dressing, pie—so keep
    The Alka-seltzer near.
A special time for families
    To meet, and eat, and pray;
Give thanks for all your blessings on
    This and every day!

December

It's time for Christmas shopping,
    For wreaths, and holly, and
Wood fires blazing on the hearth,
    As winter tips his hand.
A time of joy—a time of love,
    A time for peace on earth,
As Christians celebrate once more
    Our blessed Savior's birth.

Gardens

As winter wanes, within me always comes
A stirring, somewhat like a sprouting seed—
An urgent, even almost desperate need
To choose and buy the seed and plan my annual garden.

Each passing day with great anxiety
I watch the ever-rising temperature
Until at last I can be fairly sure
The likelihood of killing frost is finally passed.

At last the magic moment is at hand!
I know my joy, to others may seem toil;
I do so love to feel and smell the soil
Turned by my churning tiller tines.

Between two wooden stakes, I stretch my line
And space the long, straight rows according to
The detailed garden master plan I drew
One snowy day so many weeks before.

In fine, soft bed I lay my precious seed,
To sleep in warmth and peace each day and night
Until at last they all are brought to light
By sun and rain in close-knit partnership.

Each day I scan with eager, anxious eye
The daily weather forecasts I so fear,
And thrill when tiny green sprouts first appear—
my children—all conceived in faith and love.

Am I, perhaps, a fool to plant so soon?
I know that I indeed have tempted fate,
And pray that errant, killing frost this late
Will not destroy my labor done in love.

Of course, no garden ever is pure joy;
All gardens have their share of urgent needs . . .
Cultivate at times and hoe the weeds,
Fertilize and water when the rain is not forthcoming.

Tomatoes must be firmly staked and tied—
Kentucky Wonders must have climbing poles,
Then fight the groundhogs, rabbits, squirrels, moles,
Plus cutworms and a hundred other insect pests.

Since self-maintaining gardens don't exist,
There's lots of work and worry there for sure;
Hence, aches and pains all gardeners endure.
Hot baths and liniment are most gardeners' dearest friends.

No, gardens aren't for prim or lazy folks
Who never in their lives have really toiled,
Who dread to get their hands or clothing soiled.
For work, and sweat, and dirt are what a garden's made of.

Why then do folks so willingly subscribe
To sunburn, backache, blisters from their tools?
It almost seems all gardeners must be fools!
If so, then many very happy fools there be.

If they are fools, then count me first among them.
Few greater joys in this great world I know
Than to plant such tiny seeds and watch them grow
Until they give to us of food or beauty.

The garden that this world has long known best
Is Eden, hence we know that it is true—
God is a dedicated gardener too!
And who would dare to say that God's a fool?

Likewise, the Son loved gardens also, for
The night before he died on Calvary's tree,
Christ prayed in the garden called Gethsemane.
Yes, gardens may just be the ideal place for prayer.

I spend a lot of quiet time in gardens,
And not alone, for God is also there.
In gardens, joy prevails against despair,
For seeds of hope and faith and love and joy
Grow very well in gardens.

When life's problems,
Worries, trials o'erwhelm you,
Find a garden to work in, walk in, be in—
Maybe just to sit and think and pray in.
I truly believe you too will find God there!

April 5, 1992

Church garden started by the author and Milton Sanford on Sanford family property paid medical expenses for church members and needy people in the community of Mount Juliet, Tennessee. In the garden were approximately 400 tomato plants and a huge variety of vegetables, all hand-watered from a horse trough of rainwater.

This poem and others were written on Evergreen Lake (first photograph and also pictured on the cover). The lake was frequented by the author's fellow teachers from Normandy High School in St. Louis County, Missouri, and by members of the support group also mentioned in the introduction to The Sharing.

Siege of the Seasons

Though the odds have long been hopeless,
Fall battles to the last,
The valiant leaves succumbing
To winter's icy blast.

Each sees his comrades falling
By the hundreds all around,
Till he in turn is wounded
And tumbles to the ground.

Formidable this foe they fight,
And certain to prevail—
Armed to the teeth is winter,
With wind, snow, ice, and hail.

Airborne the enemy attack—
Cloud bombers, wave on wave;
Fall watches as her soldiers fall—
Powerless to save!

Briefly the fallen thrash;
Each with his final breath
Settles in some sheltered spot,
There slowly claimed by death.

The battlefield is littered with the dead—
Still winter's legions go—
On total victory bent . . .
Annihilation of the foe.

Ranks decimated, ragged in defeat,
Fall leaves the field;
Leaving here and there in ash and oak,
Brave souls who will not yield.

Long is the siege that lies ahead,
And most will finally fall,
Their struggle spent to no avail—
Most, perhaps but not *all*!

Some there may be who will
Yet welcome ally spring,
And only then yield place in line
To replacements she may bring.

New legions of leaves, sore needed,
Forcing winter to retreat,
Turning the tide of battle,
Salvaging *victory* from defeat!

Autumn, 1962
Evergreen Lake

Top: Evergreen Lake silhouette; bottom, aerial photo on postcard published by R. Hostkoetter Photo Co.

Caw

Duck hunting was my favorite sport,
But when the season ended,
I missed this sport so very much,
Dark clouds on me descended.

I used to hunt for lowly crows
But then things changed, you see.
They changed quite suddenly beneath
A big old hickory tree.

I saw a black lump on the ground
Beneath that big old tree;
A lump not there the day before.
I thought, *How could that be?*

I hurried there to check it out.
To my surprise I found
A baby crow too young to fly
Huddled on the ground.

I picked him up and took him home.
I asked him what his name was.
As I stared in total awe,
He very clearly answered, "Caw, Caw, Caw!"

He had a way of finding me—
Some *sixth* sense, I guess,
Because I would disguise myself,
To deceive him, I confess.

Sometimes I'd put son Doug's clothes on
To fool the bird that day,

But that ruse too would fail to work,
He'd find me anyway!

To this day, I've never shot another crow—
It might be Caw!

Always an animal lover, the author had a pet crow (tamed but free in the wild) named Caw that would fly down onto his shoulder, no matter how many different caps and jackets he wore to try to fool the bird or how many other people were in the field or the garden.

Caw would stand on the top rung of a stepladder, with the family cat sitting on the rung just below him. Sometimes Caw " played" on the ground with a dog. Other critters rescued to become part of the family were a red fox squirrel, a baby skunk, many turtles from Evergreen Lake, and numerous cats and dogs. The author once had a barrel-racing horse named Rebel, whose natural agility and speed made it easy to teach him how to herd the author's five head of cattle.

Warm Colors

The joy is great for him who strays
Through painted woods on autumn days;
For it's now, o'er all the land,
That nature waves her magic hand—
Touching every poet-heart
With the splendor of her art!
Absurd the thought that such a plan
Be ever matched by mortal man
On canvas, with colors of his own making.

In the fore, the mighty oak
Stands proudly in his royal cloak,
And sturdy hickories and ash
Crochet a brilliant, yellow sash.
Stunted oak and sassafras
Blaze fiercely in an orange mass,
Showering down their flakes of rust
Before November's sudden gust
Of frost-kissed, nose-nipping wind.

Christmas Is a Magic Time

Christmas is a magic time,
With Santa Claus and toys;
Christmas is a magic time
For little girls and boys.
And Christmas is a magic time
For all the grown-ups too,
Despite the fact there's lots of work
And things they have to do.
Cleaning, shopping, cooking,
Are work, you must agree;
They have to hang those outdoor lights—
Put up the Christmas tree.

Christmas is a joyous time,
When we hear the church bells ring;
Christmas is a joyous time
When we hear the carolers sing.
There's joy at Christmas dinner,
As we bow our heads for grace;
There's joy in opening presents—
Joy on every face.

Christmas is a holy time;
Three wise men saw a star;
Remembering the prophecy,
They followed it afar.
It led them to a stable where,
On simple bed of hay,
Wrapped tenderly in swaddling clothes,
The blessed Christ-child lay.

Christmas is a loving time,
This is what God intends;
Christmas is a loving time
For family, neighbors, friends.

Yes, Christmas is a loving time—
His gift from Heaven above;
Another word for Christmas . . .
Quite simply: Love! Love! Love!

Choir Rehearsal

A wide array of clothing—
Bright colors, every hue;
Assorted skirts and blouses—
Slacks—sweaters, old and new.
The colors dominating
For Christmas, reds and greens;
Most, dressed for comfort only—
Some even wearing jeans.
And what a fun occasion
This practice seems to be,
With friendly, festive air
Of informality.

But come each Sunday morning,
How different things appear,
Replacing smiles and laughter,
A solemn atmosphere;
So solemn in procession—
Such solemn robes as well—
So solemn in demeanor—
Now solemn anthems swell.
Since God is always watching
(And always listening too),
For him, I have a question
When service Sunday's through.

I think I know for certain
What answer is in store—
A joyous God will answer . . .
He likes *rehearsals* more!

Christmas Anthems

Approaches fast the Christmas season
    With its myriad of joys:
Christmas trees and Christmas candles—
    Christmas lights and Christmas toys;
Christmas cards and Christmas cookies—
    Holly wreaths and mistletoe—
Skaters' fires, burning brightly,
    Casting shadows on the snow;
Sweet aromas from the oven,
    Wafting through the kitchen door,
Christmas sights and Christmas fragrance—
    All of these and many more.

But it seems to me, each Christmas,
    That the greatest joy abounds
In those things my ear enhances—
    Yes, I love the Christmas sounds!

There's the crackling of the yule log—
    Jolly Santa's "Ho-ho-ho,"
And children's happy voices
    As they frolic in the snow;
The tinkle of the small bells,
    Rung by Santas on the street,
And the frantic, urgent shuffling
    Of late shoppers' weary feet.
I love the age-old carols
    That the carolers always sing,
And to hear them oft-repeated
    Each time the church bells ring.

Most of all, I love at Christmas,
    Hearing joyous anthems swell—
Falling on each ready heart,
    Casting wide their magic spell.

And I am back in Bethlehem,
    Beneath the wondrous star,
Where star (and angel anthems)
    Drew the wise men from afar.
And since the blessed birth that night,
    No man need be alone.
My heart, each joyous Christmas,
    Sings an anthem all its own!

December 20, 1986

Christmas Thanks

As Christmas once again draws near,
We thank you, Lord, for things most dear—
Your special blessings from above—
Among the many things we love;
The joy and peace that Christmas gives,
For Christ was born, and Christ still lives!

After Christmas

Have you noticed, before Christmas,
When decorations first appear,
How they all seem bright and festive,
Adding to your Christmas cheer?
Christmas trees seen through the windows—
Holly wreaths on every door—
Festoons of pine in many places—
Christmas lights and many more.

But the first day *after* Christmas,
Though decorations still appear,
They have somehow lost their luster
As we await the coming year.
With Christ's birth, there came a promise
That God, the Father, made—
Though the symbols soon may tarnish,
Let their meaning never fade!

IV. The Sharing

A support group, attended primarily by men and women who were having marital problems or were recently divorced, met weekly at a church in north St. Louis County. These poems emerged from the sharing of their struggles, learning to cope with pain, finding hope again, and rebuilding their broken lives.

The Sharing

This long year past I've lived alone
In agony that must atone
For all mistakes I may have made.
But then I found I was afraid
To venture out and live again.

More and more I found that I,
Unbelievably, was somewhat shy!
It seems that year of doubt and hurt
Made me again an introvert,
As once I was so long ago.

I asked myself, "How can this be?"
It really is quite hard to see
How anyone who thrived on fun
Could suddenly all pleasures shun,
To stay at home and grieve alone.

So I resolved right then I would
Make serious efforts, for my own good,
To seek out friends, both old and new;
And I have since found several who,
Like me, were lost in deep despair.

And it would seem, indeed, to me,
That misery does love company,
For, in sharing here our grief,

We found a measure of relief—
Without intent—most helpful therapy!

Our bond has grown, now sisters, brothers;
We've helped ourselves by helping others.
Through look, through thought, through work, through touch,
We share the love we need so much,
And so, through love, we live again!

All bear the pain that others wrought,
Until we find the peace we've sought.
And we all dream of that day when
That special love stirs us again,
And joy is more than just a word!

Love-Talk

I've felt the soft caress of April's breath,
    Scented by spring flowers.
I've watched the long-stemmed daffodils
    Rhythmically nodding their yellow heads in the sunlight.
I've watched the turtledoves in their paired flight
    And listened to their love-talk.
On the lake, teal and mallards swim and feed—
    Always by twos.
A sturdy fork of a Jonathan apple tree,
    Holds two robins sharing enthusiastic home construction . . .
Reminders all, that spring was made
    For love and lovers;
And I am all alone!

But love will come again,
    For I still live,
And life and love, to me, are one!

Goddess

Who is this nymph with skin so fair,
With vampish smile and golden hair?
Long, burnished strands of fine-spun gold,
Like Godiva in that tale of old.
A Venus body—plain to see,
Such vision could not mortal be!
Some unknown goddess lost in flight
From Mount Olympus' lofty height.

Cheer Up

Hey, pretty girl,
Don't be so *down*—
A lovely face
Should wear no frown.

Just hang in there
A little while—
Relax a bit
And show a smile.

The days ahead
Will surely bring
All the signs and
Joys of spring.

And soon will come
One sunny day
When doubt and hurt
Will fade away.

For God has joy
For you in store
And you will laugh
And love once more!

The Cure

Yesterday I cried a lot,
Because of something I had not.
A sad, sad day because, in fine,
I did not have a Valentine!
Bitter! All her precious charms
Now enclosed in *other* arms!
Miserable, because, you see,
I spent the day in pitying me!

But gradually, as time went by,
The realization came that I
Should be ashamed to so negate,
But rather, should appreciate
The things I *have*, and so define
The many blessings that are mine;
Nature's beauties still abound,
God's handiwork is all around.

And, furthermore, I thank him too,
For giving me such friends as you!
Who subtly, somehow impart
The only cure for a troubled heart—
By word and deed, by look and touch,
Convey the love I need so much!
For my broken heart, the healing's slow—
(No wonder drugs) but now I know . . .

Though endless seem dark clouds above,
The light will come through faith and love!

February 15, 1983

V. Jack's War

Jack served in the U.S. Army in World War II and spent twenty-seven months overseas in the Pacific Theatre. He attended OCS (officer candidate school) in Brisbane, Australia, and was commissioned as an infantry officer. Prior to OCS, he served as a private in the Signal Corps. (While attending Western Signal Corps School in Davis, California, many of his military poems were published in the camp paper under his pen name, Sandy.)

Jack desperately wanted to be transferred to a combat unit overseas. After he made many requests for a transfer, a military doctor deliberately "left his glasses at home" so as not to see the disqualifying red A-X, for a minor disability, which ordinarily would have prevented combat duty. The author spent many hours overcompensating for his disability until he was finally sent overseas.

Travelogue (St. Louis to Sacramento)

Through mud-splattered windowpane of our swiftly moving train,
I watch with fascinated eye the scenes of grandeur passing by:
Missouri with her Ozark rills, her wildflowers and her wooded hills,
And Muddy Waters' yellow flood lapping at our very wheels.

The Show-Me State flies quickly past, the plains of Kansas follow fast—
Mile after mile of new-turned soil, representing weeks of toil;
And now and then a field of grain, lured to light by recent rain—
A counterpane in green and brown.

It seems but moments that I close my eyes, but suddenly I realize
That I have been asleep for hours.

And now our lazy smoke-trail drops through valleys, over mountaintops—
Through canyons, over snow-fed creeks, tumbling down from white-crowned peaks—
Colorado, land of majesty!

All too soon it is behind, and snow scenes linger in my mind
Long after Wyoming's plains unfold;
No wooded slopes or valleys lush, just seas of sage and rabbit brush.
And there the sage has washed away, revealing banks of rusty clay.
No more to Wyoming, except perhaps, like railroad lines as shown on maps,
Miles of barbed wire!

And Utah offers little more—the sage sea endless as before,
Until the vast salt wastes appear, and Great Salt Lake draws swiftly near;
Its sunlit waves of varying hue, now jade green, now turquoise blue.
A morbid beauty—here no living thing, save seagulls high on tireless wing
In fruitless search of food in that dead sea.

It's sweet relief Nevada brings; Nevada, land of *living* things!
Cattle graze on grassy hills; fertile valleys, greener still.
Horses raise their curious heads; small streams loll in sandy beds.
Haughty mallard drakes feed among the willow brakes,
And tall white cranes stand motionless on slender, yellow legs.

Faintly outlined in the western light, the Sierras tower in majestic white—
Portals to a land of charm, where *hearts*, as well as *days*, are warm,
And where, they say, the sun shines every single day;
Always a refreshing breeze, perfumed by the orange trees—
Sunny California!

Through mud-splattered windowpane of our swiftly moving train,
I've watched with fascinated eye these scenes of grandeur passing by—
At least it *seemed* that we were standing still, and all this passing by
Like moving pictures!

My Chapel

There's a chapel where I worship,
    Every hour, every day—
Where I hold my own communion
    In my own distinctive way,
And it's just around the corner
    From wherever I may be;
Although I roam the world around,
    It's always near to me.

The door is always open,
    And God is always there;
I feel his presence close to me
    As I talk with him in prayer.
I could not live without it,
    For, you see, it is a part of me—
This chapel—is the chapel of my heart!

There's a chapel where I worship—
    God hears my every word;
My troubled heart finds comfort there,
    Just knowing that he heard.
So when my days are cloudy,
    And I don't know what to do,
I meet God in my chapel,
    And the sun comes breaking through.

The door is always open
    And God is always there;
I feel his presence close to me
    As I talk with him in prayer.
I could not live without it,
    For, you see, it is a part of me—
This chapel—is the chapel of my heart!

Note: The author wrote "My Chapel" one Saturday in Sacramento, California, as he was waiting for the weekly servicemen's dinner held at Westminster Presbyterian Church. He was seated on the steps of the California State Capital building, directly across from the church. He read the poem at dinner that evening, and it was well received. Several weeks later, he was finally shipped overseas and landed at Milne Bay, New Guinea. The first Sunday he was there, he attended a church service in a quaint thatch-roofed chapel with coconut log seats. The first thing the chaplain said was, "Men, I want to read a poem written by a young soldier back in California." The author almost fell off the coconut log when the chaplain began reading "My Chapel." The poem preceded him across the ocean!

Some fifty years later, the words were set to music by accomplished musician and recording artist Tim Hayden, and the song was recorded and sung by country music star Jim Ed Brown on two Nashville television shows, the morning show, Crook and Chase, *and* Channel 4 Magazine.

The Dit-Dah Blues

Some say I am a tenor,
Some say I am a bass,
But it really makes no difference—
Can't sing in either case!

No, I'll never be a singer
For I can't tell *mi* from *fa*,
And I'll never be a code-man,
For I can't tell *dit* from *dah*!

There is no doubt about it—
At crooning I'm a flop,
Yet I'd rather be a crooner,
Than a gosh-darn *Radio-Op*!

Sandy

13 December, 1943
Code Class W.S.C.S., Davis, California, at thirteen words per minute (seventeen wpm required of code-men).

The G. B. (Goldbrick)

He woke up Monday morning with pounding head,
And while others stood reveille, he stayed in bed.
On Tuesday, his feet hurt, and he was afraid
That he *just couldn't manage* the evening parade.
He missed orientation on Wednesday night,
And on Thursday that pain in his tooth was a *fright*.
With a backache on Friday, he couldn't GI—
With every attempt, he *thought he would die*.
Saturday morning he called me a fool
For wasting my time by going to school.
When athletics are scheduled, he's far from the gym,
And there's never a Saturday inspection for him.
At last, it is Sunday—he'll sleep all the day,
For he's completely worn out . . . *from running away*!

18 January, 1944
Sunday K.P. – Davis, California

A Soldier's Dilemma

I had thought to buy you a bracelet,
But that's out of the question, I fear,
For it's quite a long while until payday,
And besides, there's no jewelry store here.
I next thought about candy,
But the story's the same as before . . .
I've searched and inquired all over,
And I can't find a candy store!
There was still time to wire some flowers,
Yet I found the same problem there too.
You see, there is no Western Union,
So I'm sending these words to you.
Yes, it's only a scrap of paper,
But of a sort that cannot be bought,
For, though these sheets may be ten for a penny,
A million can't buy the thought!

1944 – APO (Army Post Office) 703, Milne Bay, New Guinea

Precipitation

It rained like hell on Monday—
Tuesday was the same;
Wednesday, it rained cats and dogs—
Thursday, the pitchforks came.
The clouds busted wide on Friday,
And we couldn't see the ground;
Artificial respiration Saturday—
Five guys almost drowned!
This is Sunday morning—
There's a rowboat passing now,
But boats are for officers only,
So *we'll* have to swim to chow!
This is New Guinea . . .
Damn!

27 July, 1943 – APO 703, Milne Bay, New Guinea
Note: GIs were told that this was the second rainiest spot on Earth.

The Rumor Monger

"We're going to Blah; we're going to Blank—
I hear that the carrier Tuna Fish sank.
The Nth was wiped out in the Battle of Lo—
MacArthur's planning a knockout blow.
There's a new secret weapon the Japs have got—
From what I hear, it's plenty hot!
Here's a bit of inside dope—
Hitler's in Rome to talk peace with the pope.
We'll all be home in '44—
Then again, it might be four years or more.
We'd never have been here if I'd had my say—
Now the colonel told me the other day . . .
We're moving up! We're moving out!"

Hear the loudmouth yonder shout;
Some think he's really on the ball—
To most he's just a know-it-all.
Predictions he makes move right along—
Joe E. Blow is never wrong.
It matters not how things may go,
He'll always say, "I told you so!"

5 August, 1944 – APO 503, Oro Bay, New Guinea

In the late 1940s, Frank Sinatra and the Mills Brothers recorded a song titled "Paper Doll," which soared to the top of the charts. It was written by Johnnie Black, a pianist, who augmented his income by boxing. His girlfriend ran off with another boxer, and he wrote this song, which began, "I'd like to buy a paper doll that I can call my own . . ." and ended, "I'd rather have a paper doll to call my own than have a fickle-minded real live girl." But, sadly, Johnnie Black, a hard-luck guy, never knew his song (published by Carlin America, Inc.) became a huge hit; he died seven years before it caught on.

No Paper Doll

Most girls are fickle-minded,
But there are still a few
Who, despite the wear of passing months,
Remain completely true.

A paper doll or dream-girl
Might satisfy some guy,
But I'll tell you now, I'm not the one,
And here's the reason why . . .

No paper doll, however cute,
Can match a live doll's charms,
And no dream-girl, however real,
Can fill these empty arms!

No paper doll or dream-girl
Can thrill me through and through.
I gotta have a real live girl,
And that, my dear, means you!

10 February, 1944 – Code class, W.S.C.S, Davis, California

I'm Dreaming

Here on this coral island,
As Christmastide draws near,
My memories are haunted
By dreams of yesteryear:

Of cheery Christmas windows
On crowded, downtown streets,
And the hustle and the bustle
Of a million hastening feet;
Christmas carols and church bells—
Of holly and mistletoe,
And the joy of children's voices
As they frolic in the snow;
Of a thousand sweet aromas
From the open kitchen door—
Of candlelight and hearth fires,
Pine needles on the floor;
Of greeting cards and ribboned gifts—
Of laden Christmas trees,
And, oh, so many other things
Just as dear as these.

Though all these things are only dreams,
This year they'll have to do,
And I'll just go on dreaming,
For they tell me dreams come true!

December, 1943

1943 – Sketch of a dreamer under the palm trees on Biak, Dutch New Guinea, made by a company clerk named Jackie (last name not remembered), who illustrated Sandy's poems.

Pfc.

When I became a Pfc.,
    The world was looking up for me;
Just briefly I forgot to gripe
    Now that I had that single stripe.
Short-lived my joy, for I soon found
    This was the rank most kicked around.
The privates now would envy me
    And looked askance with jealousy.
From NCOs, more work in store—
    Of that one stripe, expecting more;
Since I was labeled 1st Class now,
    Far fewer goofs would they allow.
That bit of rank of which I'd dreamed
    Was not as great as it had seemed.
Assuredly, the time was ripe
    To buck hard for another stripe!

7 April, 1989

Private Jack Riehl, 1944 (age twenty-two), in the Army Signal Corps. Units of Riehl's 7th Cavalry Regiment (1st Cavalry Division) guarded General Douglas MacArthur's headquarters and family.

Corporal

I knew a long-time Pfc.
    Who thirsted for authority,
And when a corporal he became,
    Berating privates was his game.
He turned deaf ears to honest gripe . . .
    A despot with another stripe.
Just two plain stripes upon his arm—
    Then . . . Simon Legree in uniform!
He raved and ranted, threatened, swore;
    This man was rotten to the core!
For his recruits the days were long,
    Since everything they did was wrong.
Pure hate from those from his command—
    From those above, just reprimand.
At last he came to realize,
    He held the rank that all despise.
It was not like he thought 'twould be—
    Far simpler to be Pfc.

Sergeants

When I was just a private, by
    My personal rule of thumb,
Sergeants were a worthless bunch,
    And almost always dumb!
When I went through basic training,
    We had a Sergeant Burke—
(His name was really Burkens) and
    We labeled him a jerk.
He showered us with insults, both
    Direct and indirect;
He cursed us constantly and then
    Complained of "no respect."
This Burke was one example, and
    Just one of quite a few
Uncouth, sadistic sergeants that
    This hassled private knew.

When I became commissioned and
    I got my first platoon,
I didn't know which way was up
    And sang a different tune.
Sure, I attended OCS,
    (in ninety days, a wonder)
But when I gave my first command,
    I made a major blunder!
A sergeant I had not yet met,
    Foreseeing my disgrace,
Ad-libbed a clever cover-up,
    And so let me save face.
And this was not the only time
    (yes, there were many more)
that clever sergeants covered me
    Until I learned the score.

I knew a lot of sergeants in
    The span of my career,
And many times they saved my neck
    By covering my rear.
As to specific details, these
    I do not care to tell,
Let's simply say they saved the day.
    (One saved my *life* as well.)
They held it all together, and,
    Through them, the war was won;
Salute them now, all sergeants, and
    God bless them, every one!

Louies

All louies think they're wonderful—
    Some even think they're God;
In truth, it's common knowledge that
    Most of them are odd.
Now every louie hates fatigues,
    But each one loves his *pinks*;
In pinks he is the cat's meow
    (at least that's what *he* thinks).
Of course they always know it all—
    They string themselves along;
They're members of the Perfect Club,
    And perfect's never wrong!
In ninety days of OCS,
    They learned how to salute;
Methinks that time were better spent
    In learning how to *shoot*.
No doubt there's magic power in
    That gold or silver bar,
So send us lowly privates home . . .
    Let louies fight the war!

Note: Pinks are pinkish-gray dress slacks worn with a dark green short coat.

Rank

Rank has its privileges, they say,
    And this is very true,
But don't forget in judging that
    It has its duties too!
I used to envy stripes and brass
    And bucked my level best,
Moving ever up in rank
    By rising to each test.
I thrilled to each promotion, but,
    Each time, I quickly found
There, one above me yet
    To order me around.
So now I envy none at all,
    For it's quite plain to see
That, after all, *civilian* is
    The only rank for me!

Where Go My Clothes?
(or Statement of Charges)

(With apologies to Robert Louis Stevenson's "Where Go the Boats?")

Muddy is the river; muddy is the sand.
They flow along forever with tents on either hand.
Green fatigues a-floating, socks swirling in the foam—
Clothes of mine a-floating, where shall all come home?

Away down the river and on passed the ridge—
Away down the valley and under the bridge;
Away down the river a hundred yards or more,
Some other forlorn GI will bring my clothes ashore!

25 July, 1944 – APO 703 Milne Bay, New Guinea
(On salvaging a fatigue hat from the flood.)

Poison

They call it coffee!
Potent stuff—a cross between
Jungle juice and kerosene:
Stronger far than any alcoholic drink,
By taste compared with a cheaper grade of ink!
Thick as tar, and just as black.
Why not simply boil the sack
And use the contents as insecticide?
Or spray the darn stuff far and wide?
Then all GIs would show elation—
No Atabrine for the duration!
Old anopheles would be ill-fated
And very soon annihilated.
"Coffee" is what the labels show
and some guys drink it, but this I know . . .
It *isn't* coffee!

4 August, 1944 – APO 703, Milne Bay, New Guinea
Note: Atabrine *was a pill taken daily to prevent malaria.* Anopheles *is the mosquito that carries malaria.*

On GI Biscuits (or "Ingenuity")

I spread some butter on the thing
And tried to take a bite;
I put a corner between my teeth
And bit with all my might!
My incisors couldn't scratch it—
Next, my bicuspids fail;
I gnashed my mighty molars—
All to no avail!
The solution dawned quite quickly—
The biscuit's there to stay;
With a file, I fashioned a set of plates
And threw my teeth away!

27 July, 1944 – APO 703, Milne Bay, New Guinea

On Bully-Beef

Bully-beef for supper,
Bully-beef at noon,
But don't you be discouraged;
We're having steak real soon!
Red steak, rare steak—
Fit food for a fightin' man.
Almost forgot to tell you,
This steak comes in a can . . .
Labeled Bully-beef!

27 July, 1944 – APO 703, Milne Bay, New Guinea
Note: Bully-beef was a salty, Australian canned beef served in mess tents throughout the Pacific Theatre during WWII.

"The Chow in This Unit Is Terrible!" (A Story)

Lieutenant Clark and his military staff were sent to Hollandia, a base farther south than Milne Bay, New Guinea. A whole new cadre moved in. As Christmas approached, the chow seemed to be getting worse day by day. Finally the new CO, a captain, called me to the orderly room.

"Riehl," he said, "the chow in this unit has been terrible lately. Lieutenant Clark told me that you could be depended upon. I have my suspicions about the problem, but I don't want to be the one to upset the apple cart. I don't want to know what, who, when, where, or why; I just want the problem solved. The supply sergeant has orders to give you anything you need.

The next evening I stood watching the poker game in the mess tent when one of the cooks left the tent and headed back into the jungle. I followed him at a safe distance. He stopped at a large brush pile and carefully lifted the top limbs to expose what some of us had suspected for a long time—a still. He drained off about a pint of jungle juice, added some dehydrated potatoes and apples to the kettle, and headed back to camp while I followed, noting various landmarks. The next day I went to the supply sergeant and drew out a candle, a can of lighter fluid, one M1 cartridge, some twine, and a hand grenade. The next day, while all the cooks were busy, I sneaked back into the jungle, following the previously-noted landmarks, to the still. I soaked the twine with lighter fluid and gunpowder, tied the grenade handle down with the twine, pulled the pin on the grenade, and laid the grenade on the still. I placed the candle next to the grenade and lit the candle carefully. I returned to camp by a roundabout route and was watching the poker game again when the muffled boom sounded back in the jungle. The chow improved immediately.

Signs

It matters not which way you look, you'll always see a sign—
"Wear your leggin's after five," or "Take your Atabrine";
"Roll your sleeves down," "Wear a hat."
"Don't leave paper where you sat."
"Use repellent every night," "Wear your shirt or lose the fight."

You can't escape—I'll tell you why . . .
Every single time you try,
There's a sign reading "Off Limits!"

7 July, 1944 – APO 703, Milne Bay, New Guinea

Government Issue (GI)

Those shoes on your feet were made to last—
Your leggin's and cartridge belt too,
And though hell's fire be all around you,
That jeep will bring you through.
The M1 in your hand there—
That hand grenade you hurled;
Yes, you fightin' son-of-a-gun,
Your GI's the best in the world!
The steel in your helmet's the finest,
And your bayonet's tempered true,
So you take care of your GI, soldier,
And your GI will take care of you!

28 July 28, 1944 – APO 703, Milne Bay, New Guinea

Beachhead

We stand in silence on the deck.
    (The smoking lamp is out.)
The tenseness grips us, every one,
    Until we want to shout.
We clamber down the swaying nets.
    (Thank God, the sea is calm.)
Above, outlined against the sky,
    The chaplain reads a Psalm.
All heads are bowed in silent prayer.
    The loading now is through;
The push-off comes, the engines roar;
    We head for rendezvous.
We've done this thing three times before,
    And every one was tough,
But this one really has us tight;
    On nerves, it's really rough!

A breeze springs up and in the east
    A hint of dawn's first light;
The boats have reached the rendezvous,
    And now they circle tight.
Each man must face the task at hand
    And try to clear his mind
Of thoughts of home and family
    And sweethearts left behind.

At LD now with boats abreast,
    H-hour approaches fast.
Each man tries not to wonder if
    This day will be his last.
The big guns roar from ships offshore,
    The clouds reflect each flash,
And death roars by us overhead,
    Then lands with thunderous crash.

The guns on shore return the fire
    And death comes back our way.
How many brave men will receive
    Death's *calling card* today?
A big one screams by overhead
    (thank God, another miss)
with impacts all around us now.
    Can hell be worse than this?
The second hand takes one last jump,
    H-hour is at hand,
And idling engines roar to life—
    It's all out for the land!
A last deep breath, a final prayer,
    A voice says, "This is it!"
The LCs jolt against the bank . . .
    With pounding hearts, we hit!!

Note: LD is the Line of Departure from which the Landing Craft (LCs) take off for the beach at H-Hour.

Air Raid

I lie on this New Guinea shore
    Just trying briefly to ignore
War's traumas—laying them aside,
    Relaxing with the swelling tide.
What does tomorrow have in store?
    No moon tonight and that bodes ill;
The odds are good the damn Nips will
    Take their favorite midnight ride
And prove my worries justified,
    Especially since the night's so still.

Now from the north, a distant drone—
    No doubt a raid meant to atone
For daylight raids we flew today;
    Reprisal this, without delay.
And then, at last, the searchlights shone,
    Knifing through the black of night,
Penetrating to great height;
    Five *Betty bombers* cruising high—
Right now so peaceful to the eye,
    Caught in those fanning beams of light.

Expectantly, we wonder why
    Our flaunted ground guns don't reply.
Jap's target—airstrip just beyond.
    And now our Ack Ack *does* respond—
A million tracers arch the sky.
    In awe we watch the bright display,
Entranced, held spellbound by the fray.
    And now the dreaded, screaming sound
Of bombs descending to the ground.
    And we, till now, forgot to pray.

Moved by the instinct to survive,
    To earth we GI foxes dive.

Ground quakes with each and every boom—
    Thunderous is the voice of doom,
Louder the voice to stay alive.
    The bombs have stopped; still time to die—
For death still flies—I'll tell you why . . .
    This aftermath is always bad,
Like bees or hornets, fightin' mad,
    Spent shells and shrapnel whistling by.

The turmoil lessens by degrees,
    But acrid smoke still taints the breeze.
Our visitors, now homeward bound,
    Their mission done with no planes downed.
It's time to check for casualties.
    Near miss, on anchored ammo ship,
Some craters on the landing strip;
    Torn and flattened tents abound,
Just one plane damaged on the ground,
    But not a casualty this trip!

Unscathed are we, miraculously,
    Not even minor injury.
A special blessing here we share,
    So at this time, in silent prayer,
We all, Dear God, give thanks to thee!

Sniper

Corps declares our sector cleared,
    So no more Jap attacks.
For many weeks we've stopped them cold;
    At last we can relax.

I lounge against a towering palm—
    A balmy sunny day,
And I am back at home once more;
    The war seems far away . . .

It's Sunday morning, time for church,
    A day in early spring,
And everyone is ready now.
    Church is a family thing.
Dad's wearing his new navy suit,
    And Sis is wearing blue;
Mom has her flowered bonnet on,
    And I am pin-neat too.
We park the Ford behind the church
    And meet the Bowmans there.
I smile at pretty Janet, but
    That's simply all I dare.
Processional is over now—
    The choir stands up to sing
And *she* is in the second row—
    She is the sweetest thing!

The choir director's ready.
    The two white candles glow;
The organist begins to play
    The prelude, soft and low.
The melody is lovely; then . . .
    That foreign sound—a crack!
Both choir and Janet vanish and
    Abruptly I am back!

Our B.A.R. man cuts a burst
    From behind a crumbled wall,
And from a palm tree to my left,
    I see a body fall.
I hear a sound beside me now,
    A kind of sighing sound,
A rifle slides from his limp hand
    And Joe slips to the ground.
Blood-bubbles fleck his mouth and chin,
    Surprise shows in his eye;
In disbelief and agony
    I watch my buddy die!

Note: B.A.R. stands for Browning automatic rifle, which was the smallest fully automatic infantry weapon. Normally, every infantry squad (usually twelve men) has one B.A.R.

Aussies

I spent some time *down under* and
    It took me quite a while
To make a real adjustment to
    Their spoken language style.
Fair dinkum and *Good on ya, maite,*
    First seemed a bit contrary,
For, though I looked, I found them not
    In any dictionary.
But language was no barrier—
    Before my stay was through,
I found out, to my great relief,
    They spoke some English too!

I visited the USO—
    Was destined soon to meet
Two young and lovely ladies there,
    And both of them were neat:
Long-limbed, blonde, athletic Claire
    (We danced up quite a storm);
In contrast, tiny Paddy who
    Just effervesced with charm.
And soon I came to understand
    How a GI could decide,
With home-fires faint and far away,
    To take an Aussie bride.

The Aussie men—a rugged lot,
    Most often lean and lank,
And openly resentful of
    The well-heeled, "bloody Yank."
The underlying friction there,
    Quite obvious to all,
Occasionally resulted in
    A rather bruising brawl.
But all of this was put behind

    Quite willingly when we
Left Brisbane's pubs to face at last
    Our common enemy.

New Guinea, Moresby, last defense,
    Their homeland to protect;
Those Aussies held against all odds,
    And gained the world's respect.
Then on to island hopping,
    Such was the allied plan;
With GI flanked by Digger now—
    The world's best fighting man.
Just one encounter hand to hand,
    And someone near me cried,
"I love those wild men over there . . .
    Thank God, they're on our side!"

Reminiscing

Dedicated with love to Mr. and Mrs. Will Vogt; their son, Bob; and their little girl, Jean: a truly Christian family, living in Sacramento, California, whose home is what a home should be.

Home, you want to go home, you say,
To that little white house across the way;
The house with the hedges, row on row,
The house with the garden where hollyhocks grow;
The house with the big yard and carpetlike lawn
That the gang used to play croquet upon,
The yard with the low fence and creaky gate,
That *tattletaled* when you came home late;
The house with the long porch,
The porch with the swing,
Where the neighbors' kids gathered
To gossip and sing;
The house with the birdbath and flagstone walk
That leads to the door that seems to talk,
Saying, "Just wipe your feet on the welcome mat,
And come right in and hang your hat."

Each of the rooms is a study in art,
Each is a picture that's dear to your heart;
The living-room windows with curtains of lace,
Your favorite chair by the fireplace;
The piano right where it used to be,
With the same old ivories out of key;
The crowded bookshelves, books old and new,
The old-fashioned sofa with room for two;
And Grandmother's china cabinet in
The dining room there,
With its hand-painted china
And worn willowware;
The same tipsy chair at the table—
The table with sliding top;

The bloomed-out begonias on the windowsill
From the corner flower shop;
The swinging door to the kitchen—
The kitchen so cheery and bright,
With the icebox in the corner
That you raided every night;
The butter and meat are missing now
That were inside before,
And the cookie jar is empty now
Behind the pantry door;
The front burner still leaks
On the gas stove, the old toaster is falling apart—
The drain in the sink's still half-stopped up,
And that leg on the table's still short.

Remember the squeak on the stairway
(It's the third from the top stair that squeaks)—
The stubborn lock on the bathroom door
And the hot water faucet that leaks?
On the floor beside the bathtub,
The old bath mat is growing frayed,
And at the frosted window,
The same temperamental shade.
Through the open doorway,
Just across the hall,
You can see the room in detail
In the mirror on the wall;
The delicately curtained windows,
The half-opened closet door,
The quaint and tidy dresser,
And the soft rugs on the floor;
That lamp on the little table,
That darn alarm clock on the chair,
And those timeworn bedroom slippers
Just as you left them there;
The huge cedar chest beneath the window,
The blue coverlet on the bed,

The bed with the downy mattress
And twin pillows at the head.

Home, you want to go home, you say,
To that little white house across the way,
"Tomorrow, soldier, we'll all go home,
Never again the world to roam;
And you'll stride right over the welcome mat,
And you won't get a chance to hang your hat,
For *someone* will be waiting there
At the open door,
And you'll have her close
In your arms once more!"

Work! Fight! Live! Pray!
For *that* moment . . . and *that* day!

Sandy

Note: Begun in Sacramento and completed at APO 503, Oro Bay, New Guinea

The Saga of 'Nam

(In 'Nam)

We fight a war best not begun;
    I quote from poet Tennyson:
"[Ours] not to reason why—
    [Ours] but to do and die!"
And die we do and for a cause
    Of doubtful merit. Conscience gnaws,
But military law demands
    That soldiers follow all commands;
So day by day we go along,
    Sometimes in actions that seem wrong.
Agent Orange gains renown
    By changing jungle green to brown,
And pity those who raise a fuss
    By asking what it does to us.
And what a hopeless task have we,
    Fighting those we cannot see,
An enemy that rates us fools
    For our attempt to follow rules.
Deceit and guile, their specialty—
    Yes, every kind of treachery!
The toughest part, we all agree . . .
    Identifying enemy.
Alert each moment, day and night,
    Note any sound, however slight.
Observant always, this could be
    Dear Charlie walking next to me.
You've heard the quote, but let me tell
    You . . . this war's far, far worse than hell!
At home, they're demonstrating there!
    It's only right that all should share.
Since they're so eager to attack . . .
    Send them to 'Nam, and we'll come back!

(At Home)

At last we're home—our ordeal's through;
    But no, for all those tales were true!
We gave our best, we shed our blood;
    Then came home to a bitter flood
Of criticism, blame, and hate!
    Don't we deserve a better fate?
Those dirty looks most all the time—

    Folks calling what we did a crime.
We did some things against our will,
    And conscience nags us sometimes still,
But, after all is said and done,
    It's still a fact that wars aren't won
By strict adherence to the rules
    And those who think so are just fools.
We all endured such deep despair;
    Friends gave their lives up over there,
While those at home, our efforts spurned,
    The flag we fought for, *others* burned!
Where'er we go, those looks so cold,
    And others even much more bold.
It's hard to believe such hate was spawned
    That we are cursed and spat upon.
Are these acts freedoms that could be
    Meant by the word *democracy*?
All other wars brave heroes make,
    But we, our country does forsake.
Feel our sorrow, hear our plea—
    Don't let us live in infamy!

11 November, 1991

VI. The Lighter Side

Wolf

When he says he's glad he's found you,
If he says, as he is bound to,
That he's mighty glad he's found you,
And he slips his arms around you,
Baby, he's a wolf.

If he parks his little flivver
Down beside the moonlit river,
And you feel him all a-quiver—
Baby, he's a wolf.

If he says you're gorgeous looking,
That your dark eyes set him cooking,
But your eyes aren't where he's looking,
Baby, he's a wolf.

When he says you're an eyeful,
And his hands begin to trifle,
And his heart pumps like a rifle,
Baby, he's a wolf.

If by chance when you are kissing,
You can hear his heart a-missing,
And you talk but he won't listen,
Baby, he's a wolf.

If his arms are strong with sinew,
And he starts the gypsy in you,
So you want him close against you,
Maybe, Baby, *you're* the wolf!

Note: A flivver is an old or cheap car.

Pianos

Pianos are so versatile—
    They have so wide a range
In octaves, and, like vintage wine,
    They mellow some with age.
In tone as well, they're versatile
    (Don't need to tell you that)—
Hit white key for a normal note,
    black key for sharp or flat.

As far as *type* of music goes,
    Pianos have pizzazz;
Versatility here too—
    From classical to jazz.
Just think of the variety
    With which we have been blessed—
From chopsticks with two fingers to
    Concerto, Chopin's best.

Pianos have endeared to us
    So many favorite airs;
I always loved pianos, till—
    I moved one up the stairs!

1986

Chiropractor

The waiting room, though almost filled,
    Is quiet as the grave;
A thin façade on every face
    To show that they are brave.
A sweet voice calls my name at last
    After quite a lengthy wait;
My time has come! With shoulders squared,
    I go to face my fate!

I follow her obediently,
    On down the narrow hall,
To tiny torture chamber
    With weird pictures on the wall
Of skeletons, perhaps of those
    Who did not quite survive,
And silently, I breathe a prayer
    That I'll come out alive!

First off, I get the ultrasound
    Or other treatment suited;
I grit my teeth and pray once more
    I'm not electrocuted.
And now the moment dreaded most
    (The worst is now in store) . . .
A subtle sound out in the hall,
    And he walks through the door!

A fiendish look is on his face;
    He stares with icy eye;
Indeed, some ice surrounds my heart;
    I fear that I shall die!
No hesitation on his part—
    He puts me on the rack.
I know his silent battle cry:
    Attack! Attack! Attack!

"With this manipulation, I'll
    Your vertebrae align."
This sadist is determined to
    Annihilate my spine.
He spends the next ten minutes, then,
    In *pretzelizing* me;
My arms and legs are bent to where
    Men's limbs weren't meant to be.
At last the ordeal's over, and
    Not one time did I balk.
Amazingly, I *did* survive,
    And I can actually walk!
What utter fools we mortals are—
    Indeed, it is unreal
That voluntarily we submit,
    And pay for this ordeal!

Practitioners they're sometimes called;
    Once, witches bore this name.
It's logical the name's still used;
    Their deeds are much the same!
So horrible, these deeds they do,
    Let's modern law forsake,
Just do as our forefathers did,
    And burn them at the stake!

Postscript:
The mind of man is fickle though—
    Should pain relief come soon,
We soon forget all these complaints,
    And sing a different tune.
God alone works miracles,
    And this we know for sure,
But chiropractors often work
    Some most amazing cures!

Pigs

Most folks think pigs are ugly—
For the most part, I agree,
But *little* pigs are really cute—
As cute as cute can be!

They bounce around like rubber balls
And utter high-pitched squeals;
The only times they settle down
Are nap times and at meals.

Pigs, of course, just love the mud—
One finds it; others follow.
That is when the party starts—
Just wallow, wallow, wallow!

Our kids also like the mud
And every mother knows it.
The only difference I can see . . .
The human kids outgrow it.

Pigs' eating habits should explain
The reputation they have gotten;
Their table manners aren't the best,
In fact, they're downright rotten!

Now pigs and rabbits share some fame,
And I'll be more specific . . .
Pigs like most kinds of rabbit food,
And both are quite prolific!

It's plain that pigs and rabbits are
Very amorous critters;
Quite simply, this explains, you see,
Their large and frequent litters.

The thing that I like best 'bout pigs
I think that you'll agree,
Is the table fare that they provide . . .
Great versatility!

For breakfast, there is sausage—
A terrific food, I think,
And even here there is a choice
Of patty form or link.

And then, of course, there's bacon,
A special treat for me.
Therefore I think that I will choose
For lunch, a BLT.

For dinner, friends, the choice is tough.
I dearly love pork roast,
With potatoes, carrots, onion, and
Gravy . . . that's *the most*!

But there's another dinner choice
I also think is tops,
Sizzling in the frying pan . . .
Those golden brown pork chops.

Sausage, bacon, roast, and chops—
Prepare them as you would,
So here's to pigs, despite their faults . . .
Because they taste so good!

February 24, 1997

Cheetah

Shrewd killer of the jungle,
Swift killer of the plain,
How many hapless creatures
In your lifetime have you slain?

How many speedy victims
Have you dragged down in full flight,
Then bloodied up your jowls on,
As you gorged throughout the night?

And when hunter became hunted
For your prized, soft, spotted skin,
The odds seemed stacked against you
In a game you could not win.

For the bullets could o'ertake you,
Despite your blinding speed;
In this contest of survival,
You would all your cunning need.

My Cheetah is a hunter too—
She stalks around the house,
Slaying moths and other game,
And once she slew a mouse!

At Christmastime she climbed the tree,
As hunting cats will do;
And there she worked pure havoc . . .
Ten ornaments she slew!

Yes, she's a mighty hunter,
But I will tell you that,
She's also quite a lover—
My little Cheetah cat!

Mother-in-Law

(Fictional)

While driving into town one day,
    I stopped for lunch along the way.
A certain waitress caught my eye,
    And when she brought the menu by,
She smiled at me. What can I say—
    She simply took my breath away!
Eyes, deepest blue; blonde curls galore,
    Soft, sexy voice, and so much more;
So well-endowed, tight-fitting jeans—
    A body like I'd never seen!
I got her name—phone number too—
    Just two quick dates before I knew . . .
She was *the one*, I had no doubt,
    That all my life I'd dreamed about!
A home-cooked meal by candlelight—
    The food she served was sheer delight.
Proposal followed—sat up late;
    She said, "I do." We set the date.
The wedding, then, was set for June,
    And it could not arrive too soon.
We wed and then she dropped the bomb . . .
    This was the first I'd heard of *Mom*!
No honeymoon of bliss, you see,
    Ours was a honeymoon for *three*!

My marriage had just one big flaw,
    For with it came a mother-in-law!
Mother-in-law, mother-in-law,
    With it came a mother-in-law!

-2-

My marriage was, indeed, ill-fated—
    Not what I had anticipated.

The first week disillusioned me—
    'Twas nothing like I thought 'twould be;
We'd go to bed, turn out the light—
    I'd reach for her 'most every night,
And always came the voice of doom—
    "No, Mama's in the other room!"
Each day that passed, I seemed to find
    New things to which I had been blind.
Each morning she veneered her face,
    And glued false lashes into place.
Blue eyes were contacts, feet were big__
    And when she put her nightie on,
    I wondered where those curves had gone!
Then came the words I'd dreamed about . . .
    "Guess what? Mama just moved out!"

My marriage now had one less flaw . . .
    For I was rid of my mother-in-law!
Mother-in-law, mother-in-law!
    I was rid of my mother-in-law!

        -3-

How could I know what lay in store—
    Came revelations by the score.
A single day was all it took
    To find out that she couldn't cook—
Made coffee either weak or strong;
    Everything she did was wrong.
The eggs were hard, the toast was burned—
    For Mom's return I promptly yearned.

My marriage still had one big flaw . . .
    For now I missed my mother-in-law!
Mother-in-law, mother-in-law,
    I really missed my mother-in-law!

My darling wife could see no wrong
    In watching soapies all day long.
She couldn't cook, she couldn't sew;
    She *did* know how to spend my dough.
I did the wash, went to the store—
    Then washed the dishes, swept the floor.
Eight hours a day I worked like hell,
    Then slaved at night at home as well;
With constant nagging day and night,
    Since nothing that I did was right.

My marriage had just one big flaw . . .
    I should have married my mother-in-law!
Mother-in-law, mother-in-law,
    I should have married my mother-in-law!

February 12, 1990

Mashed Taters and Squirrel Gravy

(Fictional)

Now I was born in twenty-two—
    The Great Depression, I lived through.
A hilltop farm in Tennessee
    In boyhood days was home to me.
My chores were many, times were hard . . .
    Fix the fences, mow the yard;
Then every spring, the garden plow,
    And plant, and hoe, and water now.
Always vegetables to eat,
    Beyond our budget, though, was meat.
The orchard gave us fruit and honey.
    Tobacco patch brought some cash money.
For change of menu once a week,
    I'd catch some catfish in the creek;
And sometimes when my chores were through,
    I'd load my trusty .22
And take my younger brother Bill
    To Hickory Grove up on the hill.
A little luck and I was able
    To put *real* meat upon the table,
For very seldom would I fail
    To bag at least one bushy-tail.
And our reward for such a feat,
    A very special family treat—
A big ol' pot of squirrel stew
    With carrots, onions, taters too.
The young and tender ones, Mom fried
    To golden brown, and on the side
To put some meat upon our bones . . .
    Mashed taters and squirrel gravy!

It's natural thus to reminisce
    Despite my present life of bliss.

Today I have a loving spouse
    And own a nice suburban house;
Big hickory trees, a lovely yard,
    And times right now are not so hard.
With stylish clothes, not overalls—
    Some classy artwork on the walls.
A far cry from Ford's model T,
    Two late-model cars have we.
We pay our bills as they come due,
    And can afford a trip or two.
We even save a small amount.
    No plowing here, no aching backs;
Retired now—time to relax.
    Relax, indeed, though chores are gone . . .
And sport a modest bank account.
    Indeed, life now is hard to beat—
Including super things to eat—
    Shrimp and lobster, juicy steak
At fancy restaurants on the lake.
    Such food is great, beyond a doubt,
But sometimes still I dream about
    Squirrel browning in the pan, and . . .
Mashed taters and squirrel gravy!

One thing I did not count upon;
    A complication in our life,
Quite suddenly beset by strife.
    Squirrels here and squirrels there—
Squirrels galore, so many that
    It frustrates our poor tabby cat.
Squirrels hopping, scolding 'round the place—
    She's not alone; I tell you true—
They have us frustrated too!
    As if *we* trespassers be.

I planted bulbs—they didn't sprout—
    Those sneaky rascals dug them out.

This year, no apples, for, you see,
    They ate the buds right off the tree.
Then came the deed that really hurt—
    They ate our tulips for dessert!
They thump at dawn upon the roof,
    Our bloodshot eyes are solid proof
Of damage done. Now hear the facts . . .
    We've both become insomniacs!
Day by day the onslaught grows,
    Again they've added to our woes—
On the house itself they gnaw;
    I deem this the final straw!

This time they've really gone too far;
    From here on out, it's all-out war!
No qualms of conscience—deed is done—
    Today I bought a pellet gun!
From boyhood days, a simple plan—
    The only good squirrel's *in the pan*!
Now suddenly our outlook's bright,
    Our dinner menu for tonight—
My mouth is watering at the thought of
    Mashed taters and squirrel gravy!

March 17, 1990
Note: A new generation of squirrels was gnawing the front of the Riehls' cedar siding house. With permission from the sheriff, the author, at age eighty-seven, was wielding a shotgun in a new, all-out war against the squirrels. From August, 2009, to June, 2010, his count was forty-five bushytails, and the problem was apparently resolved.

VII. Finding Love Again

The story of how my wife, Carol, and I re-met thirty-three years after I taught her ninth-grade English class is a miracle story.

One of Carol's high-school friends had heard from Carol that she was flying to St. Louis and renting a car to visit her father, who was seriously ill. Her parents lived in Iberia, Missouri, about a three-hour drive from the airport. I asked her friend to have Carol phone me when her plane arrived in St. Louis. When Carol telephoned, I offered to drive her to her parents' place. She was the same conservative, cautious young lady I remembered. Her answer: "But I haven't seen you for thirty or more years; I don't really know you."

We compromised. We agreed to meet at an airport coffee shop so she could decide what to do. I apparently passed the test, because I not only drove her to Iberia but also drove her to her home in Nashville, Tennessee. I rented a teardrop trailer and fished in Percy Priest Lake over the weekend, driving back to St. Louis on Sunday afternoon to substitute teach the following week. I proposed to her three weeks later.

-JLR

Autumn Love

A spark was struck so long ago
But never fanned, as we both know.
On separate paths for all these years,
By God's grace now your face appears.
Life's deepest grief we both have known;
Now suddenly this grief has flown.

In golden autumn of our days,
God shows the magic of his ways.
His plan . . . we two should meet, and then
Our eyes and hearts should touch again.

That tiny, ancient spark still glows;
Now, fanned at last, it grows and grows.
For certain, it's God's destiny . . .
This love of ours was *meant to be*!
Resist not that decreed above,
Now let it flame at last . . . our love!

Miracle!

Miracle!

Out of the darkness, a miracle!
After the heartbreak of the past,
Came a glimmer of hope at last;
The moment you walked through that door,
I knew I wanted to live once more.

Miracle!

I have witnessed a miracle!
Such a vision of loveliness—
My heart skipped a dozen beats, no less.
And that was the magic moment when
I knew that I could love again.

Miracle!

I have been blessed with a miracle!
From that very first moment I knew
That I was falling in love with you,
And prayed from that moment to God above
That he would let you return my love.

Miracle!

My prayer was heard, and soon I knew
That the magic of love had touched you too.
Miracle! Miracle!
The love we share is a miracle!

The Gift

I'm sending a little token
For you to remember me by—
That is, if you care to remember
Such a scatterbrain as I.
It's not an expensive present,
Nor one bought for a dime,
But it's one that will last forever,
Unaffected by wear, tear, or time;
For it's of a type of *mettle*
That dampness can never rust,
And it has a kind of working-part
That can't be clogged by dust;
A gift which might well please a king,
But such a simple, common thing.
And an Indian-giver I'm going to be,
For I ask that this gift be returned to me;
It's a hand-me-down from my Father,
My Father above!
You see, I'm sending you—my love!

Tears

I remember how it used to be . . .
    I bumped my head or skinned my knee,
And Mother came without delay
    To kiss the tears and pain away.
I cried a lot when I was *three*!

"Dear, does it hurt?" "No, I'm just fine."
    A Band-aid and some Iodine . . .
I grit my teeth and lived the lie
    That "big boys never, never cry."
I was so brave when I was *nine*!

Then next there came the football scene—
    And I was rugged—I was mean,
So tough, indeed, that I decline
    The Band-aids and the Iodine.
Oh, macho me at age *sixteen*!

Then came the day I took a wife;
    With ease I bore all pain and strife.
Her gentle words and loving touch
    Could soothe all hurts so very much . . .
But suddenly she left my life!

Near always once, but now she's not—
    Our sacred vows, somehow forgot.
In second childhood then, you see,
    And no one there to comfort me,
So, once again, I cried a lot!

New love I've found, my life to bless,
    And we two share our hurts and stress.
In total candor I will tell,
    Occasionally, the tears still well . . .
Now blended in togetherness,

  But always now they're tears of joy!
Tears, still tears,
  But tears of joy!

July 12, 1986

You

I thought my life was over once,
But I was wrong, you see.
You walked right through the door one day,
And became the world to me.
    You!

You are the robin's morning song,
The sweetest song he sings;
You are the pastel bluebell
That fills the woods in spring.
    You!

You are the brightest rainbow
That ever arched the sky;
You are the harvest moon in full;
The summer sun on high.
    You!

You're all the dreams I ever dreamed,
The heart within my breast—
A generous gift from God above,
By whom I have been blessed.
    You!

By day and night I thank Him for
This precious person who
Brings life and hope and joy to me—
This angel-person . . . *you*!
You, you, you!

Yours

My body's not a castle,
In fact, my aching back
Most certainly would indicate
It's just a crumbling shack.
My breastbone's split and hurting;
I have a patched-up heart.
Indeed it is quite obvious,
I'm falling all apart!
My mind is also going,
In fact, for all intent
And purposes, it has already *went*.

Considering all the facts above,
It's very plain to see—
My shadow is the wholest part
That now is left of me.
I don't know who would want me,
But if by miracle you do,
Every tattered, battered part of me
Still belongs to you!

Proposal

Along life's winding pathway,
Along life's maze of aisles,
Come *walk* with me!

About life's countless problems,
About life's untold trials,
Come *talk* with me!

Of happy home and children,
Of fortune and of fame,
Come *dream* with me!

Toward all those things we dream of,
Toward all our highest aims,
Come *plan* with me!

For all life's rich and real rewards,
For all life's true success,
Come *work* with me!

In all life's deepest sorrows,
In all life's happiness,
Come *share* with me!

Through all the golden years of youth,
Through silver years of age,
Come *live* with me!

Until life's chapter's over,
Till death shall turn the page,
Come *love* with me!

Rainbow's End

There was a time, not long ago,
    When all my words were tales of woe,
And each day added to my grief.
    In vain I searched to find relief;
You see, I sought it here below.

And in those days so dark and long,
    I wrote a verse, a "Rainbow Song";
A verse of hope for all to share—
    A verse of faith that God *did* care.
The proof is now—I was not wrong.

My pain was eased as time went by;
    He heard my prayers and *did* reply.
Above . . . I found my answers there.
    Yes, miracles are wrought through prayer;
This, many know as well as I.

The sun was bright, the clouds had flown,
    And in the east a rainbow shone.
I did not find a pot of gold—
    Much greater treasure did unfold.
A kind of love I'd never known!

This love I found . . . at rainbow's end!

June 15, 1986

Carol

I met her one September day
    So many years ago.
An English class, first day of school—
    Fifth seat, second row.

The roll was called and she looked up
    A moment to reply;
Her eyes met mine so briefly then,
    Her answer, soft and shy.
The finest student in the class—
    This, not to my surprise,
But what I have remembered best . . .
    Those soft, yet piercing eyes.

And since those magic high-school days,
    Until we met again,
A span of thirty years has passed—
    I was her teacher then!
Two years ago . . . a miracle,
    A golden moment when
God lifted us from loneliness,
    And let us meet again!

And had those long years changed her much?
    They'd changed her—yes, and how!
A slender, quiet student then . . .
    A stunning woman now!
Indeed, the years had changed her, but
    One thing remained; you see—
The moment that I saw those eyes,
    I knew her instantly!

Enchanting eyes of softest green,
    Yet penetrating too—
Magnetic eyes that draw your gaze—

Then look you through and through.
Laughing eyes, gentle eyes,
    That hold you in their spell;
Eyes that look into your heart,
    And touch your soul as well.

And I intend to look into
    Those dear eyes all my life;
God wrought a second miracle,
    And Carol's now my *wife*!

A wedding kiss.

Mr. and Mrs. Jack Riehl, leaving the church after wedding.
March 29, 1986.

My World Is Where You Are

Darling,
You came into my life and suddenly,
    This old world was no longer like it used to be.
The good Lord sent you down, my life to bless,
    For the first time, I knew the meaning of togetherness,
And just like that I knew—
    My world is where you are!

Those dear eyes looked right through into my heart, and then
    I knew beyond all doubt I was in love again.
The spell you wove about me was indeed too much;
    This old heart surrendered completely to your touch
And now I know . . .
    My world is where you are!

Every time you're even close to me,
    Everything seems just the way it ought to be;
And always, when we two are far apart,
    I try in vain to sooth an empty, aching heart
With thoughts and dreams of you.
    My world is where you are!

And when you're lying close to me at night,
    I know that nothing else has ever seemed so right.
Ours is a close and everlasting bond.
    We'll be together always—in this world, and beyond,
So love me ever, leave me never for . . .
    My world is where *you* are!
Yes, my world is where you are!

March 29, 1990

Home

I love this house!
That's what I've always said;
Now suddenly I find
It's the *home* I love instead!
These past few days
Have brought the message through—
It's really not the house at all,
But the *home* I have with *you*!

Wife Carol, author Jack, about twenty years later

Top: Lakeshore home in Tennessee (a) in springtime; bottom: (b) in winter.

Tina-Dog

We have a precious baby girl
Who has four tiny feet;
She prances to the front door
All callers there to meet.
She's our official greeter
All callers best take heed,
Our baby is a min-pin,
An alert but friendly breed.
She is a super watchdog;
She watches every day
And barks at people on the street,
A hundred yards away.
We love our baby very much
And thank the Lord above
For sending this dear baby girl
For us old folks to love!

Tina-Dog (a miniature pinscher). She was a lost dog who found the Riehls on Good Friday at a roadside campground, eating hungrily out of a Styrofoam cup. Their truck door was standing open, and she jumped into the driver's seat, turned 'round and 'round three or four times in the "bedding-down" ritual that dogs instinctively do, and made herself at home. No one claimed her, and the Riehls loved her for more than five wonderful years.

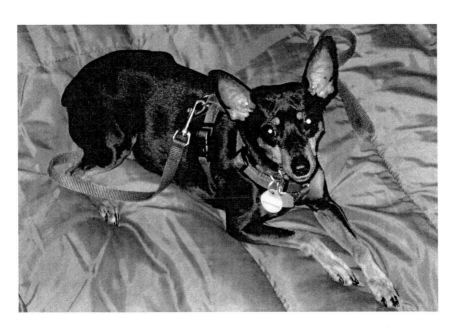

Tina Riehl (ca. 2001 - 2010)
On satiny, orange bed, wearing purple harness, collar, and leash, she won a blue ribbon in a dog photo contest.

Just before Heart and Soul *went into production, she died suddenly on Sunday morning from a tumor at the base of her heart.*
(Photograph by Leroy Humphries.)

Tessie-Cat under rocking chair. She lived to age twenty-two.

VIII. School Days

The Librarian

Who drifts through stacks and main room
With a special kind of grace?
Who talks to kids and colleagues,
A smile upon her face?
Who fascinates the fellows
With her unique and special charm?
Whose bubbling personality
Flows from a heart so warm?
Whose pretty head is full of facts
Like many of her books,
Whose covers tell just what's inside?
(This lady has the looks!)
Who turns on all the fellows
And sets their hearts awhirl?
Who? Why, who else could it be . . .
It's our little Marjie girl!!!

For Marj Courtney, Normandy High School librarian, Normandy, Missouri.

Subbing

With malice aforethought, or so it seems,
Ma Bell shatters my tender dreams.
Thus begins my joyous day
With dawn's light yet an hour away.
"Miss Jones is out at Senior High."
"Okay," I answer, with a sigh.
"Oh, yes, there's one thing you should know—
first class began ten minutes ago!"

Clothe my body, hit the street,
No time to shower, shave, or eat.
Of course just when I'm in a rush,
I hit the morning traffic crush.
In office now, I'm signing in,
Secretary, with apologetic grin:
"It seems she left no lesson plan.
You'll have to do the best you can."

Unlock the room. It's ten below,
Outside it's only zero or so.
Students standing in the hall,
Half perhaps, not nearly all.
Others, finding the door shut,
Disappear and risk a "cut."
Another handicap I find,
To total failure now resigned.
How can I even make a start
With no class roll or seating chart?
Upon the desk, the schedule there,
Instantaneously raised my hair . . .
Algebra (quantities minus, plus)
Also trig and calculus!
Those very words turned my heart sick;
I barely passed arithmetic!

And thus began six hours of strife—
The longest day in my whole life!
I tried those impish minds to reach—
God knows I really tried to teach!
What mischief did their minds contrive;
Content now I just to survive!
Ten hands raise—requests galore—
To lockers, guidance, nurse, and more.
The whole day long with no abate—
"Restroom, Teach—I just can't wait!"
Six hours of pain, six hours of hell;
Oh, blessed was that final bell!
And fool I am indeed, I guess,
Asking for that kind of stress.
After tolerating all that racket,
I'm ready for my own straightjacket!
Now finally comes the realization . . .
It's obvious, no *ifs* or *buts*,
Beyond a doubt, I'm just plain nuts!

Life's lowest form, beyond dispute . . .
The trod-on high-school substitute!

Swan Song

Five years ago I said farewell
    And shed a tear or two;
The tears may flow again today . . .
    Once more I say adieu!
And many, many memories,
    Both good and bad, are mine,
And many friends have come and gone
    Since 1949.
To those of you who still remain,
    And those departed too,
I thank you for good memories
    And leave some love for you.
But *most* of it (my love, that is)
    I take along with me
And give it to a lady down
    In Nashville, Tennessee.
How young she was when first we met
    In East 286;
Today it seems that fate has played
    One of its nicer tricks.

My years here end at thirty-eight,
    And that is quite a span;
My room today . . . 286,
    Right back where I began!

April 24, 1987
The author subbed for the last time in Room E-286, Normandy High School, Normandy, Missouri., having retired from full-time teaching five years previously.

IX. Fields and Streams

The author was given a rifle at a very young age; he loved to go hunting and fishing with his dad, Walter, who was an expert trap shooter. This love of the outdoors prompted Jack to buy Evergreen Lake and later an adjoining farm in Illinois. Over the years, he envisioned and developed this land and lake into a licensed, fee-fishing lake and campground.

Fish-Bit

One day I went a-fishin'
    And soon got lost in thought;
I sat there just admiring all
    The fish that I had caught.

I found myself a-thinkin'
    How cruel this world can be—
I took that dandy string of fish,
    And let them all go free!

It was just a weaker moment, though,
    And not my normal plan—
I usually take those rascals home,
    And cook them in a pan!

September 2, 1987
Percy Priest Lake, Nashville, Tennessee

Trout Fisherman

I wade the noisy riffles, and
    I fish each quiet pool,
Applying all the knowledge gained
    In Isaac Newton's school.
And so, with each and every cast,
    My mind anticipates—
Behind each rock and eddy there,
    A wary rainbow waits.
That tree root there, a likely spot—
    A lunker there may lie,
And as I cast, a shadow moves,
    And rises to the fly.
No rainbow this, but monstrous brown;
    To every jump, I thrill;
For fish and fisherman, a test
    Of instinct, strength, and skill.
A veteran of many wars—
    Of this there is no doubt;
Up close, at last, I now can see
    His scars from other bouts.
At last I lead him to the net—
    Admire him briefly, then
Release him, gently as I can,
    To rise and fight again.
A pause, and then he darts away—
    Both pounding hearts abate;
Upon a rounded boulder near,
    I sit and contemplate.

I find a balm of solitude—
    Feel worldly pressures less;
Yet, with God's creatures all around,
    There's never loneliness—
Blue heron waiting patiently
    For food to come its way—

Kingfisher poised on barren limb—
    A pair of mink at play.
No human voice or telephone
    To spoil my reverie;
Just music—water, wind, and birds—
    A woodland symphony.
No time clocks are there here to punch—
    No deadlines here to meet;
No customers, no bosses,
    No competitors to beat.

I write my own prescription here
    For worry, stress, and pain—
Prescription proven, oft renewed,
    Yes, *fishing keeps me sane*!

October 1, 1987

Blue heron. (Photograph taken on Old Hickory Lake, Tennessee, by Carol Lefmann Riehl.)

Jack holds up a thirty-pound buffalo fish he caught on an ultra-light rod out of Couchville Lake, Long Hunter State Park, Hermitage, Tennessee.

The Hunter's Reward

A roar of wings, the covey springs
    Into the frosty air.
Two shots resound, two birds are downed—
    And feathers everywhere!

Dove Hunter

I stand, a statue in the dawn,
With head turned toward the sky,
And thrill at sight and whisper of
Small phantoms passing by.

I load my pump—three lethal loads—
Put down my coffee cup;
Three feathered jets are coming fast,
And now the sun is up.

The action's fast; the barrel is hot,
And when the hunt is through,
I'll have a *hundred* empty shells—
Perhaps one bird or two!

September 1, 1987

X. Armchair Philosopher

Eagles

Hear now this earthbound poet's words,
    Expounding on the king of birds.
He soars on pinions, broad and strong,
    Effortlessly all day long,
Observing all, with practiced eye,
    The world below that's passing by.
He plummets down then, swift and hard . . .
    Success, at last, is his reward.

Strength and stamina, patience too,
    All these, the eagle shows to you.
Achieve new heights, take time to soar,
    Then, like the eagle, climb some more.
The world is yours if you aim high,
    But you'll not know unless you try.
God made the eagle with delight,
    And you are greater in His sight!

July 24, 1988

Gossip

Do not pass them on
    When petty things are said
But think on them instead,
    Until it's clear to you
That they're completely true;
    And, even then, hold back.
Although they may be true,
    Still, damage they may do.
Words often go awry.
    Better to let them die
Than to offend.

Four-Letter Words

Not only is it most unfair,
But also quite absurd,
To judge without impartial trial
The poor four-letter word!

The naughty ones, you know about,
So these, I will not mention,
But those so often overlooked,
I'll bring to your attention.
There's *kind* and *fair* and *glad* and *give*—
There's also *work* and *play*;
There's *nice* and *good* and *like* and *care*,
And *help* and *hope* and *pray*.

And number one of all such words,
That gift from God above—
The word that makes the world go 'round—
Again, four letters . . . **Love**!!

Pronouns

There's this and that and who and whom—
There's also he and she.
There's which and none and anyone—
There's you and I and me.
And then we have the plural forms—
There's more and most and all.
There's these and those and they and them,
And some I can't recall.
Why dwell on all these parts of speech?
(For so it does appear)—
It's far from my intention
To teach some grammar here.

Most pronouns deal with people, and
I hope to make you see
The two of most importance are
The pronouns *us* and *we*.
We . . . you and I together,
(Now, that really is a plus!)
Objective forms—the same is true,
For *you* and *me* make *us*.
Though "Pronouns" is the title of
This verse, I do confess . . .
The thought I *really* have in mind
Is just *togetherness!*

The Surgeon's Prayer

Lord, clear my mind and take me to
    The limits of my skill.
Please let me feel your presence near
    And the guidance of your will.
Don't let success inflate my head,
    But keep me in my place;
For my success is your success—
    It's you who grant me grace.
And help me, Lord, to justify
    All those degrees I've earned,
And confidently put in use
    The knowledge that I've learned.
So guide my hand and touch my heart,
    And let me forget never
That in this world, it's you who are
    The *greatest surgeon* ever!

December 27, 1995

Fashion

Now there are those who are obsessed
With how they're groomed and how they're dressed.
We're all aware that there are those
Who spend a fortune just on clothes,
And also spend a goodly share
Of money, just to style their hair.
This big obsession is, I guess,
Simply to their friends impress.
And every year the fashions change,
But this is really not so strange,
When money in such large amounts
Swells designers' bank accounts.

For those who care how they appear
But can't afford new styles each year,
There's one thing you can always wear,
And of attention draw your share.
This item doesn't cost a dime
And can be worn just *any*time;
It's highly valued for this reason,
And it's in style in *every* season!
Summer, winter, spring, or fall,
Wear it anywhere at all;
For you will always be in style
If you will wear a smile!!

Note: This poem, written many years ago, is hereby dedicated to a beloved friend, Ellie Schmidt, who always had a beautiful, contagious smile, no matter her circumstances. Even when she had tears in her eyes, she would smile. She smiled (almost all the time), joyous or sad; in the hospital, in pain; in hospice, and at the very end of her life. She died February 1, 2010, trying to cheer up everyone around her.

Book of Life

I thumbed with idle fancy
Through the book which I had bought,
And wondered how many others
Had shared with me the thought
That *life* is a book.

A book with birth and death for covers,
It seems to me;
Bound in cardboard, cloth, or leather,
As the case may be,
But incidental to the content.

Days are the pages, years the chapters—
Small or bold the print;
Plain or painted the language and style,
Varying greatly by dint
Of the whim of the author.

Fiction—perhaps a novel,
Of slight value in itself,
Or a collection of facts—a huge volume
High on the reference shelf,
Or a book of poems or short stories.

Some lives, like some books, are best sellers,
Bringing success in a monetary way—
Success often doomed to be short-lived,
Completely gone in a day—
And forgotten forever.

Yet some books live on though centuries pass—
Classics, we call them then;
And some *lives* live on defying death,
As models for other men
To remember and live by.

Just a word about authors—
Books are written by men.
God alone is author of lives,
But we put ink in the pen!
Only his penmanship is flawless.

November 26, 1947

Key to Happiness

Now, I am no philosopher, as philosophers go—
No Socrates, and yet I know
That the truly happy man is he who *loves*!

Loves to work and loves to play—
Yes, who loves his very way of living.
Loves his country as his life,
Loves his home, his kids, his wife;
Who loves to sleep and loves to eat—
To put old slippers on tired feet
And sprawl in solid comfort in his favorite chair,
To relax and read his paper there;
Who loves to talk and laugh and sing—
To hear the friendly doorbell ring
And have friends crowd in through the open door.
Who loves the sunshine and the rain
Spanking against the windowpane;
Loves the daytime and the night,
Loves to read and loves to write—
To lie before the fireplace
And feel the warmth upon his face;
To sit beside some quiet stream
With nothing to do but fish and dream,
And just be lazy!
To sit in bleachers at baseball games,
And call the robber-umpire names;
To bowl with the gang on Monday night,
And be high-man if his game's just right—
To stop by the gym and get a rub,
Then hurry home and fill the tub,
And soak for hours!
Who loves the sound of people's feet
Scurrying by out on the street,
And the patter of smaller feet upon the stairs;

Who even loves the hat his young wife wears
To church on Sunday morning.

Yes, who loves all these and a million other things,
And, lastly, the promise the future brings;
And loves a generous God above
For giving all these things *to* love!

XI. Heart and Soul

My God

I have not heard his voice—
I have not seen his face,
Yet I know beyond a doubt
That he is present in this place.

I have not heard his footsteps,
Nor felt his touch of hand,
Yet, when I pray I know he hears
And that he understands.

A God whose awesome power
All evil can transcend,
Yet, to me a gentle, loving God—
A constant, caring friend.

A friend I can confide in—
My darkest secrets bare,
And one who will rejoice with me,
My greatest joys to share.

My God is *always* near me,
Not just watching from above;
My God is a *giving* God,
And his *greatest* gift is love!

Have Faith

It's Sunday, and in all free lands,
Church doors stand open wide
For those who still have faith in God
And come to worship him inside.

In other lands those doors are closed;
The pews stand dark and bare,
But tomorrow's sun will cast its light
On many faces there.

Until that glad tomorrow comes,
Each one must do his part
By keeping Jesus Christ alive
Within a Christian heart!

Pioneers

We have launched a major venture,
    Greatly favored by the odds;
We've a partner in this venture,
    For this venture's also God's!
As the church we plan progresses,
    And grows ever through the years,
Proudly may we bear the name . . .
    We are also pioneers!
This master plan was drawn up by
    That master architect above;
Hence, our faith will be the mortar,
    And the cornerstone—our love!

Foundations

To build a house, a barn, a store—
    Materials choices are galore.
First, what foundation should we use?
    There's treated wood and concrete block;
There's man-made brick and natural rock . . .
    For lasting qualities we choose.

To build a church, a home, a life,
    Which will survive all storms and strife.
One more material . . . from above:
    Foundations which will crumble never;
But set up fast and last forever . . .
    These things are always built on *love*!

February 29, 1988
(Groundbreaking, Grace United Methodist Church, Mount Juliet, Tennessee.)

Above All

If only I could dance!
If only I could sing!
If only I had talent
In any worthwhile thing!
If I had such charisma that
The girls could not resist!
If I could write a novel on
The year's best-seller list!
If I could win a scholarship
And earn a PhD!
If I could bat .400 plus
And be the MVP!
If I could gain 1,000 yards—
The Heisman Trophy win!
If I could shine in any field
And feel that glow within!

We cannot all be famous and
We cannot all excel.
What counts is not just what we do,
But that we do it well!
Whatever gifts God gave to you
(With love we are all blessed),
Just take these gifts and use them well
And always do your best!

God Bless You

(To my friend John, on the death of his wife.)

God bless you through the black of night,
God bless you through the day.
God bless you every step you take
Along life's narrow way.
God bless you, too, in all you do,
Be it work or play.
God bless the very thoughts you think
And every word you say.
God bless you with some happier times,
And comfort when you're sad.
God bless you when you're very good;
And again someday be glad!
God bless you with time's passing,
As the winged hours fly—
Every minute of each day,
And as the years go by!

Today, tomorrow, and forever,
May he who watches guard you ever.

God bless you!

December, 2007

Microscopic

It may be a seed or a tiny plant;
It may be a bee or a lowly ant;
It may be a mite of a hummingbird—
Just the trace of a smile, or a three-letter word;
The little finger of a baby's hand
Or the very finest grain of sand.
It may seem insignificant to you—
Perhaps one of myriad drops of dew;
However small a thing may be—
Though it's even too small for the eye to see,
It's never so small that one should flout,
For it's those little things that count!

He's There!

On darkest days, when skies are gray,
    So often we forget—
Behind the shroud of dark gray cloud,
    The sun is shining yet.
Then suddenly the sun breaks free—
    The clouds are gone and then
We realize, to our surprise,
    The blue shows through again!
Have faith! He's there!

In times of strife throughout our life,
    In times of stress and care,
Lay cares aside, in love abide,
    For God is *always* there.
Your faith renew—he'll see you through,
    So lift your hearts in prayer;
Just seek his grace in *any* place,
    For God is *everywhere*!
Have faith! Have faith! He's there!

Rainbow Song

Life's road is winding, narrow, rough;
It leads through tunnels, dark and long.
For days, and weeks, and months, and years,
It seems that all goes wrong!

And all our friends and family too
Remind us constantly
That if we just *hang in*, then life
Can only better be.
Hang in we have, as time crawls by,
And still *hang in* we do;
Hang in we will, however long,
Until our trials are through.
We doubt, sometimes, these moral friends,
But trust that Friend above,
Who promises to give us joy
And fill our lives with love.
This promise, clearly written is:
"As ye sow, so shall ye reap,"
And faith, we have in darkest hours . . .
This promise, he will keep!

At tunnel's end, a rainbow bright—
Perhaps, a pot of gold,
But certainly, a life of joy
Will for us all unfold!

Look Up!

What if the day is dreary
And dark clouds do abound—
What if the rain is falling,
And the mud is all around?
    Look up!

What if you had a sleepless night
And tossed the whole night through—
What if you did come late to work,
Then missed your ride home too?
    Look up!

What if your luck is running bad,
You're feeling sort of *down*—
What if it's hard to force a smile,
Instead you wear a frown?
    Look up!

What if you burned your dinner,
Then dropped it on the floor—
What if the hot pan hit your foot,
And now your toe is sore?
    Look up!

What if everything goes wrong
For you, day after day—
What if you're so discouraged
You threw your rabbit's foot away?
    Look up!

What if the rain keeps falling,
Snow there's now a trace—
Just smile and look up anyhow—
That rain won't melt your face.
    Look up!

The sun still shines behind the clouds,
But clouds will drift away—
Your troubles too will disappear
Some balmy, joyous day.
    Look up!

So raise your head and lift your heart,
And see the bad times through—
They say that hope's eternal—
God's eternal too!
    Look up!

Tomorrow
(A New Beginning)

Sometimes it seems that hope is gone
When all those troubles come along.
Sometimes it seems that life is through
When everything goes wrong.

A better day is coming soon—
A bright day—you will see;
Tomorrow will be better, far,
If you will let it be.

Tomorrow is the next today,
The future's not yet cast,
And yesterday cannot be changed,
So let the past be passed.

The past should be forgotten then,
With all its pain and strife;
Tomorrow is the first day of
All the rest of your life!

Long Hunter

Upon these grounds we now enjoy—
    This public park we show,
Another race, Americans too,
    Roamed many years ago.
Upon this spot what hunter stood,
    Drew gut-strung hickory bow,
And loosed his flint-tipped, feathered shaft
    At elk or buffalo?
Choctaw, perhaps, or Chickasaw,
    Beneath a cedar tree,
So patiently awaiting prey . . .
    Or was he Cherokee?

With simple weapons he performed
    Amazing hunting deeds,
And always limited his kill—
    Just filled his basic needs.
Respect he showed, in many ways,
    For land where he *did* roam,
And planned that generations hence
    Should also call it home.
A kind of reverence he had,
    Yes, reverence and love,
For One then called by many names . . .
    Creator up above.

Then came from far across the sea
    These men of paler hue,
Who killed the buffalo for sport
    And wasted timber too.
Soon certain species were extinct,
    And others faced this fate,
But finally clear minds prevailed—
    For some 'twas not too late.
Today, at last, the tide has turned—

  The battle flag's unfurled;
Now conservation is our theme . . .
  Let's work to save God's world!

April 5, 1992
Written for and read at the dedication of Long Hunter State Park's new visitor center, Hermitage, Tennessee (near Nashville).

Hymn of Creation

A wise God gazed at empty space
    And liked not what he saw;
Six days he labored to create
    A world without a flaw.
He formed the land with mountains high,
    He poured the mighty seas,
Then added color to the scene
    With grasses, flowers, trees.
This world . . . our first great gift from God!

Then God surveyed his wondrous works
    And suddenly he knew
That something still was missing there—
    The job was not yet through.
The creatures of both land and sea
    Were added to his plan;
God then scooped up a bit of dust,
    And he created man.
Life was our next great gift from God!

The eyes of God looked down at man—
    Looked long and deep within,
And saw in every human heart
    The shadows there of sin.
He sighed a mighty sigh to find
    The job was still not done,
And so he sent his dearest gift—
    His beloved only son.
Christ is our dearest gift from God!

Christ suffered, died, and lives again;
    To thus our sins replace;
God only asks that we believe
    And grants to us his grace.
The *greatest* gifts that we've received

From our Father God above,
Two gifts as dear as life itself,
    Are Jesus Christ and love.
By far, our greatest gifts from God
    Are *Jesus Christ* and *love*!

October 1, 1993
Set to music and recorded by Tim Hayden.

XII. Over the Hill

Old-Timer

Another year, another beer,
And you've begun your slide;
A bitter pill—to be over the hill,
And on the downhill side!

This year just passed, you've faded fast.
Alas, there is no cure;
Old age is so relentless—
Wheelchair's next for sure!

Has-Been

Dedicated to all aging courtsters who can remember, or at least imagine, that they once roamed the court with speed, agility, power, and a degree of tennis talent.

Right from the start I'll be up front
    And set the record straight—
Please know that even at its best
    My tennis was not great!

There was a time, however, when
    I played and felt no shame—
No pro, of course, and yet, I think,
    I played a *decent* game.
But decades pass, as decades will;
    The years, their toll will take,
And even memories grow vague
    Of shots I *used* to make.

Gone is the solid backhand stroke—
    The blistering forehand drive;
Both are wounded birdies now,
    No matter how I strive.
Old muscles fail in trying for
    Tough shots I used to get,
And now my drop shot really drops . . .
    On *my* side of the net!
Sometimes I can remember how
    It felt to serve an ace,
Now . . . just avoid a double fault . . .
    To that degree, save face.

Remember, too, how good it felt
    To *cream* an overhead,
But yesterday I set one up
    And smashed just *air* instead!

I find that I am facing now
    A truly awful fate,
For I've become the hacker that
    One time I used to hate!

Lost gradually throughout the years—
    Ability to win.
Gained slowly, learning how to lose—
    To take it on the chin.
The good Lord lets me still compete
    And win one now and then . . .
Not bad for one approaching fast
    Those threescore years and ten!

Yes, tennis is a game I love—
    A truly super sport,
So when I'm gone, please bury me
    Beneath a tennis court!

May 19, 1991
(Author's 69th birthday. He played tennis until he was at least 80 or 82.)

Think Young

In case you're counting every one,
    As years just roll along,
You may be thinking that you're old,
    But I can prove you're wrong.
I know it seems there's just no way
    To keep the years in check.
It's not the years that make us old—
    Forget them—what the heck!
For *thinking young*, I'll guarantee,
    Will make those years depart,
For nothing else defies the years
    Like being *young* at *heart*!
And here, once more, I will expose
    My ego (also id).
I have you beat by many years,
    And *I* am just a *kid*!

About the Author

Jack London Riehl taught high-school English for thirty-three years. He received bachelor's and master's degrees from Washington University, St. Louis, Missouri.

He served in the Army in WWII and Korea. He has three children; two grandchildren; one great-grandchild.

He and his wife reside near Nashville, Tennessee.

English teacher and chairman of the Basic English Department, Normandy High School, Normandy, Missouri.